MW01699984

"*The Go-Getters* is an excellent book that deserves the attention of any job hunter or university student soon to enter the job market. For an inexperienced person, it's totally out-of-the-box thinking. For an experienced professional, it's the only way to conduct a job search and manage a career.

A market-driven approach is right on the money—it transforms the typical job search into a market-savvy process. It's an absolutely essential and relevant approach for today's market-sensitive and intensely competitive job environment. Use it to find career success!"

— Gregory Sterling, Fmr. Partner, Accenture

THE GO-GETTERS

Market Driven to Career Success

Gaining a Competitive Edge in Your Job Search

THE GO-GETTERS

Market Driven to Career Success

David A. Lee

Foreword by
Scott Howard

Sierra Pacific Publishing
Rancho Palos Verdes, CA

THE GO-GETTERS
Market Driven to Career Success
by David A. Lee

Published by arrangement with Sierra Pacific Publishing,
a division of EGL Holdings, Inc.
28364 South Western Avenue, PMB 463
Rancho Palos Verdes, CA 90275 USA

Lee, David A.
The go-getters : market driven to career success :
Gaining a competitive edge in your job search / David A.
Lee ; foreword by Scott Howard
p. cm.
ISBN 0-9758607-1-2

1. Job hunting. I. Title

HF5382.7.L44 2004 650.14

Book Shepherding Services and Production Editor,
Gail M. Kearns, www.topressandbeyond.com
Cover and Interior Design, Robert Aulicino, www.aulicinodesign.com

Printed and bound in the United States.

For distribution and sales inquiries, please contact Sierra Pacific Publishing
by telephone toll free: 888-432-1176 or fax: 310-732-1176.
www.sierrapacificpublishing.com

Dedication

Dedicated to my dear mother, Evelyn Grace Lee, whose courage and support has been an inspiration to me beyond her imagination.

Acknowledgments

I would like to thank the many people who graciously assisted to help make this book a reality. This includes first and foremost my production editor Gail Kearns, copyeditor Barbara Coster, book designer Robert Aulicino, and those who previewed the book and supplied valuable suggestions and comments—Scott Howard, Greg Sterling, Dave Kiyasu, Kaitlyn Lucus, Larry Gray, and Diana Chew. I would also like to thank the many people who allowed me to interview them to gain a greater insight into the challenges of finding a job and managing a career in today's environment—working professionals, corporate managers, university students, and college career advisors. My thanks go out to all of you.

I hope each of you finds satisfaction in knowing that your contributions will enable countless numbers of people to find career success through this book.

About the Author

David A. Lee is a graduate of the University of California at Davis and has worked for multinational corporations and conglomerates in banking, telecommunications, manufacturing, real estate, and hotels. Throughout his career, as a corporate banker, business planner, and financial manager in the U.S. and Asia, David has been intimately involved in business decisions that resulted in the hiring of thousands of people.

Contents

FOREWORD

You are to be commended!

If you've bought this book, you are taking more control of your career. This is a big first step toward realizing your dreams. Now you must follow through and implement your job search.

Not an easy thing to do, however. Securing the right job takes patience, hard work, and, as David Lee points out in his valuable book, a solid plan to lead you to success.

I've been in your shoes before. After graduating with a psychology degree and a master's degree in higher education, I found work at Hewlett Packard and joined the human resources department. Later, my career flourished at Sun Microsystems, 3Com, and Asera Corporation.

Now I am living my dream in Hawaii, as a member of the executive team and head of HR for a biotech start-up.

Throughout my career, I was thoroughly involved in the recruitment and hiring process.

In my positions, I recruited graduates from top universities in the country, hired PhD engineers, and offered jobs to outstanding managers. I've considered thousands of candidates through resumes and interviews.

Finding a job when I graduated wasn't easy then, and it isn't easy now. And it's not easy for experienced workers seeking better career opportunities either.

But by using a market-driven approach for your job-hunt and career management, you will definitely have an edge. A market-driven approach will not only help you land a job today, it surely will help you maximize your career over the course of your life.

Instinctively, I've used a market-driven approach over the years to manage myself and have had a wonderful career. You can too.

David Lee has penned what I feel is a book long overdue. His guidance is extremely useful and applicable in today's market and can help job hunters of all types.

In the real world, a market-driven approach works. Whether you seek an administrative, professional, technical, entry-level, junior, or senior position, this book will help—it's smart, concise, and practical and will definitely give you a competitive advantage.

Good luck, and have a marvelous career!

Scott Howard
Director of Human Resources
Hawaii Biotechnology, Inc.

INTRODUCTION

Finding a good job is one of the biggest challenges you will ever face. For most, a good education and experience are no longer enough to secure solid employment and successful career growth.

Why? Because the employment environment is constantly changing, forcing new demands on job hunters and employees every day. What may be a great job today may be a declining job tomorrow.

On top of this, every day more fresh graduates are entering the job market, more qualified and experienced workers are seeking a career change, and more highly trained personnel are out of work searching for a new job.

As a result, in today's continuously changing and ever-competitive market, you have an important decision to make. You can look for a job just like everyone else, using traditional strategies and channels, and hope that something good arises. Or you can utilize a savvy *market-driven* career and job-hunt strategy and increase your chances of finding the type of job you want.

What happens to companies that are not market driven? They perform poorly, they lose out to the competition. The same is true for job hunters—they also lose out to the competition.

The choice should be obvious—a market-driven strategy works no matter which situation you're in:

- whether you will soon graduate from college and wish to enter the job market;

- whether you're currently employed but want a new job or career;

- whether you're forced to change jobs because of the result or threat of retrenchment.

On the flip side of the coin, the market is filled with many wonderful careers that you've dreamed about—jobs that can take you around the world, jobs that can earn you big bucks, and jobs that can provide you the satisfaction, security, and growth you need.

So, what do you do? How would you go about finding a job that fits your expectations?

How would you apply a market-driven strategy that gives you a competitive advantage?

This book may be your answer. It provides a market-driven business approach for turning your motivation into action, how to find a great job.

But this is no typical how-to guidebook, for the following reasons:

1. It's presented in a parable format, telling the stories of 10 job seekers. Any one of them could easily be you. With this storytelling style, you have a greater connection to the real-world issues that characterize the job search and how you can realistically implement a successful job-hunt strategy.

2. It's a guidebook wrapped in a short story. But it's not your standard super serious how-to book that requires days or weeks to digest. It's fresh, smart, and highly readable. You can read this book in just a few hours.

3. It's totally practical. The main theme of this book is how to use a market-driven business approach for your job hunt. This book contains real-world tips, most of which only a savvy business professional would know.

4. It's greatly focused on the job search. You know you need a new job, you've completed your self-assessment, you've updated your interviewing skills, and you've already prepared a resume. You just need a solid game plan to find new employment.

A wonderful career is waiting for you. All you need to do is reach out and grab it!

Overview

The story opens with 10 characters, called the Go-Getters, who are about to end a trekking vacation in Nepal. The group consists of five recent university graduates, four others presently working but looking for a job change, and one recently laid-off worker. Guiding the group is a retired professional and former corporate executive from Wall Street, who unexpectedly becomes their mentor.

The Go-Getters have one thing in common—they all face a challenging job search situation.

For the five recent graduates, they are woefully unaware of the issues facing them concerning the job hunt. Yet, with a diploma finally in hand, they are thrust into the market and now face the dilemma of how to successfully find a good job.

For the four currently employed, though they have a few years of work experience, they find themselves in an unacceptable working situation and are eager to change careers.

For the one who recently got a pink slip, though she has three years of experience, she faces an uncertain situation combined with emotional stress and a super competitive job market.

Compounding their collective condition is the fact that the most influential factors in their lives have provided little job planning advice. Their parents lacked wide industry knowledge to give sufficient guidance. Some didn't invest sufficient time to utilize university resources that were available. And most of their professors couldn't offer much insight, since they themselves possessed virtually no industry experience.

While all the Go-Getters are motivated to find a new job, they actually have very little idea of how to implement a successful job hunt.

Sure, they know how to prepare a resume and be interviewed, they know how to take an aptitude and a personality test, and they know how to job search using newspaper classifieds, job websites, and job fairs. But these days, almost every other job hunter knows this too.

Fortunately, they find a mentor in their trekking guide. He provides real-world, practical advice about the job market and ways to achieve a competitive advantage.

This is a story of how the 10 Go-Getters apply market-driven job-hunting advice to their respective situations.

The Go-Getters

Name	Home	University	Education	Status
Jeff	Toronto	University of British Columbia, Vancouver	Pharmacology	Fresh Graduate
Matt	Miami	University of Florida, Gainesville	Interior Design	Fresh Graduate
Carl	Philadelphia	Penn State, University Park	Accounting	Fresh Graduate
Kathleen	Chicago	University of Illinois, Urbana-Champaign	Mechanical Engineering	Fresh Graduate
Derek	Kansas City	University of Kansas, Lawrence	Business	Fresh Graduate
Erica	New York City	State University of New York, Albany	Marketing	1 Year Work Experience; Employed
Wendy	Atlanta	Georgia State University, Atlanta	Chemistry	1 Year Work Experience; Employed
Heather	Houston	Texas Christian University, Fort Worth	Latin American Studies	2 Years' Work Experience; Employed
Sims	Seattle	Lewis & Clark College, Portland	Communications	2 Years' Work Experience; Employed
Ann	Los Angeles	California State University, Sacramento	Computer Engineering	3 Years' Work Experience; Laid Off

Part I

GET READY: UNDERSTANDING THE PLAYING FIELD

Chapter 1

From One Challenge to Another

New hopes and ideas

They had just finished their 14-day trekking expedition in Nepal and were now on their way home.

Unknown to each other at the start of the trip, they had developed a special bond with one another. Learning about the unique culture of Nepal, together with the mind-boggling scenery of the Himalayas, served as an everlasting knot in their newfound friendships.

Leaving Kathmandu, they relished the experience while catching a final glimpse of the awesome terrain at the footsteps of Mount Everest.

They had each gone to Nepal for their own reasons—some seeking a well-deserved break after graduation, others wanting a vacation from careers they questioned, and one seeking solitude after being hit with a lay-off notice. All had sought discovery, in themselves and in what they wanted in their future.

With the end to their vacation, they each realized that a new challenge lay ahead of them—finding a new job.

The thought of looking for employment sends chills down the spine of most would-be job hunters.

The threat of higher unemployment rates is ever present.

Companies continue to announce layoffs. There's news of fresh graduates who can't seem to find a job. On top of that, many experienced workers are either out of work or searching for better jobs. The competition for jobs is intense.

But the Go-Getters are armed with something not taught at school: survival skills learned in Nepal. And not just mountain survival skills, but skills needed to successfully find employment.

Their guide, Sam, was not only a capable explorer but also a talented and experienced corporate manager. He had made his millions in business and decided to leave the world of Wall Street and high finance for the outdoors.

Between his tales of Nepal and its rich history, Sam also spoke from his experience as a corporate banker, financial manager, and business planner. He had worked on the East and West Coasts of the United States for both large and small companies, and overseas in Europe and Asia.

Sam clearly understood the job anxieties of the group. Not only had he been in their shoes before, but he also had been on the other side, interviewing many job hunters and making decisions about which candidates to hire and which employees to lay off.

Throughout his career, Sam had also worked in positions that involved job creation. He intimately knew the key business factors that resulted in job hiring.

He was happy to give his insights not only about the hiring process and what companies look for but also about little-known but extremely useful tips job hunters can use to find career success.

Before meeting Sam, the Go-Getters thought they were reasonably prepared for the job hunt. Some had attended career workshops at their universities, others had read guidebooks on how to prepare a resume and how to interview, and all had taken aptitude and personality tests. On top of this, they all had seen job-hunting tips in the newspapers and on the Internet.

Sam helped them realize that *finding the hiring company of their choice* was the real key to career success.

He said, "You've got to have a solid strategy. Understand that there is no magic or secret way to finding a good job."

Sam's advice was extremely practical. Sitting around a campfire one evening, Sam posed a question to the group. "Though important, what good are a well-written resume and impressive interview technique if you can't find a company in a position to hire you?"

"Not a lot," they all agreed. "But apart from job fairs, newspaper classifieds, and job websites, how do you find companies who are looking for people?" someone wanted to know.

"Well, that's exactly the type of question you should be asking," Sam said.

"Years ago," Sam recalled, "I read a book about international finance. It fascinated me. I dreamed of becoming a globe-trotting international banker. Months later I found work at **Standard Chartered Bank**, the big British bank, and was placed in the West Coast international department handling countries in Asia. Years later I sat on the beach in Los Angeles watching jumbo jets bound for overseas. I thought to myself, 'Someday I'll be on one of those headed for a new job abroad.' Soon afterwards, I became a corporate planner for an Asian conglomerate in Hong Kong, living the life of an expatriate. Both were fantastic jobs. And I didn't find either position through the classifieds or a job website."

"Hearing about my aspirations and results, a CEO of a multinational company once offered a compliment and called me a real *go-getter*.

"Jobs of your choice are attainable," Sam stated with passion. "All it takes is a little imagination, planning, and execution. And oh yes, desire!

"Anything is possible, *if you're a real go-getter*."

"Go-Getters! Yeah, we're Go-Getters too," the trekkers all shouted around the campfire.

By the end of the trek, the Go-Getters realized that they had attended the best career workshop imaginable. Sam was exactly the kind of career mentor they needed—caring, informed, and worldly. Sam opened their eyes to new hopes and ideas.

The trek had ended. Upon arriving at their transit airport, they bid farewell to one another. And everyone made sure to get Sam's e-mail address.

Chapter 2

Adopting a Market-Driven Business Approach

Like market-driven companies, job hunters can also find success

Sam's main point to the Go-Getters was simple and straightforward. He said, "When a company hires you, it's a business decision—pure and simple. It's the same in every market, whether you're in Miami, Los Angeles, Kansas City, or Vancouver."

A company that hires you considers fundamental business factors: Do you fill a need, will hiring you enhance productivity or add to the bottom line, is the market growing sufficiently, is the company optimistic in its future, do competitive factors justify hiring you, and is the budget sufficient to offer you a job?

Sam explained, "As a job hunter, you've got to understand this and adopt a business approach too. Realize that you're a product with features and benefits. You've got to find the company that needs you.

"Even when the job market is favorable, competition for good jobs is fierce," he said. "It's vital, therefore, in good times or bad, to market yourself as best as possible."

In business, successful market-driven companies understand this very well. Simply put:

- Companies analyze what features and benefits their products possess. They also analyze any weaknesses and act to mitigate them.

- Companies determine what marketing channels are the best. They decide if only a few or if several channels are necessary.

- Companies proactively seek business. They don't wait for opportunities to come knocking at the door; they take the initiative and actively seek business.

- Companies develop a marketing plan. They analyze each facet to optimize their effort.

- Companies investigate the primary and secondary industries that need their products.

- Companies don't blindly approach prospective buyers. They do it intelligently.

- Companies follow up diligently. They assume their products are needed and do their best to overcome rejection.

In good or bad economic times, companies do their best to maximize their effort. They know that competition never ceases.

Sam stressed, "As a job hunter, the same concepts

apply to you. To get ahead, your job-hunting strategy should take on the characteristics of a business strategy—you need to be *market driven*."

He asked, "What happens to companies that are not market driven? They perform poorly, they lose out to the competition, they produce substandard products, or they completely fail. The same is true for job hunters; they lose out to the competition."

To beat the competition, job hunters must

- analyze their strengths and weaknesses;
- determine which job search channels are best for them;
- proactively seek job opportunities;
- develop a well thought-out career and job search plan;
- analyze which industries are growing and provide the best opportunities;
- stay abreast of market information relevant to their career interest;
- intelligently approach prospective companies;
- follow up on each application diligently and effectively.

It is absolutely critical to recognize that job-hunting is a marketing effort that requires a solid business approach. Those who understand this will have the best chance to beat their competition, find a job of their choice, and maximize their career.

Chapter 3

Optimism Is Everything

Turning adversity into success

The second main point that Sam conveyed was to remain optimistic. He said it was vital to realize that many good jobs exist and are surfacing every day.

He said, "Even if you've been laid off or are graduating into a difficult job market, know that jobs are always available. You may have to dig a little deeper for opportunities, but they are there. Adversity doesn't create character, adversity reveals it."

Thinking especially of Ann who had just been laid off, Sam offered, "If you've been made expendable, it is absolutely critical that you remain positive. You're not the first person to ever be laid off, nor will you be the last. This happens every day. What really matters is how you deal with it.

"If retrenchment was abrupt and unexpected, you might feel depressed or bitter or lack motivation. You might even want to take some time off before you start your job search. This is entirely normal. But at some point, you'll need to face the realities of your situation."

Sam gave some suggestions:

1. **Maintain a perspective.** It will help you get through this difficult period. Perhaps the company

was financially unstable, making future advancement uncertain. Perhaps it was a dead-end company in a dead-end industry. Even if it was a great company, getting laid off isn't the end of the world. As General George S. Patton once said, "Success is how high you bounce when you hit bottom."

2. **Get control of your depression and welcome new ideas.** Losing a job can be fate's way of saying that you need to upgrade your abilities or change your employer or career. Convince yourself that the company made a big mistake and that your next company will be lucky to have you, or take action and add new skills. Positive thinking can help you reboot to a new and better direction.

3. **Take heart in knowing that setbacks happen to almost everyone, including even the highest achievers.** For example, Abraham Lincoln, one of the greatest American presidents, had his share of hard times. But through sheer persistence and determination, he eventually triumphed to attain the highest political office in America.

   Lincoln's career chronology reads as follows:

1. Failed in business	1831
2. Defeated for legislature	1832
3. Failed in business again	1833
4. Elected to legislature	1834
5. Sweetheart died	1835
6. Had nervous breakdown	1836
7. Defeated for Speaker	1838

8.	Defeated for Elector	1840
9.	Defeated for Congress	1843
10.	Elected for Congress	1846
11.	Defeated for Congress	1848
12.	Defeated for Senate	1855
13.	Defeated for vice president	1856
14.	Defeated for Senate	1859
15.	Elected president	1860

Sam said that persistence and determination are powerful tools to overcoming adversity. And just as great most successful companies want persistent and determined employees—those who can turn adversity into success.

Sam stressed to Ann, "Look to the future and learn from the past. Try to analyze why you were retrenched and if you lack essential skills.

"Realize that prevailing market factors require many computer specialists to upgrade their abilities by adding accounting, finance, logistics, customer care, or enhanced computer abilities.

"Companies today place a higher value on employees with added value skills and those who understand how their work impacts other departments and the company as a whole, in addition to their own unit.

"Nowadays, this line of thinking applies to just about every industry, entry-level worker, and experienced professional, and not just for those recently laid off.

"Just the same, if you're an air condition repairman currently employed, learning about plumbing or electrical repair will help you stay employed and give you better career opportunities."

Ann felt better. She had been so depressed since being

retrenched. But after hearing Sam's views, including the fact that even Sam himself had been laid off once, Ann realized that she has a chance to start all over again.

She was uplifted by his confidence and optimism.

Chapter 4

Limited Knowledge Can Lead to the Wrong Path

Derek decides on a direction

In Kansas City, Derek wasn't sure what type of job he wanted. He just didn't have much knowledge of the working world. But he remembered Sam's counsel that *limited knowledge can lead to the wrong path.*

Derek studied business. He knew that his education could apply to almost any industry.

He had initially thought that he could just take any job that came along. But Sam said, "Taking any job, perhaps the wrong job, could substantially hinder your career.

"Consider the primary factors that would provide you with a fulfilling career." He suggested the following:

- Will the job be rewarding and interesting?
- Will the position advance your skills?
- Will your potential be realized?
- Will you get a fair renumeration and benefits?
- Will the work environment be pleasant?
- Will the company be financially stable?
- Will management be modern and progressive?
- Will the job provide for travel, culture, or excitement?

- Will the job train you for a future business, if that's your ultimate goal?

"More than ever, it is essential to envision the key elements to a successful career path," Sam said. "I know this sounds obvious, and perhaps for some people it's extremely difficult at this stage in your young life, but without some serious consideration it's like wandering around in the forest with no direction.

"Consider the financial consequences. Some of you may have a lot of debt from your college days or other large financial commitments. Finding the job of your choice will enable you to better manage your financial situation.

Sam reasoned that with a little effort and planning, one could find a job that provides what most people look for:

- Financial rewards
- Career satisfaction
- Employment security
- Good experience
- Job training

You may not initially find everything you want, but at least you'll be headed in the right direction.

Sam spoke of a hypothetical situation that left a lasting impression on Derek.

"What if you studied graphics design and aspired to work for an international advertising organization like **Saatchi & Saatchi** or **Young & Rubicam**, but your father's business contact found you a marketing job in a steel pipe company? What would you do?

"If the job market is tight and you have a limited financial situation, or if you don't want to put your father in a potentially embarrassing position, you might just take the job.

"If you stay at this company long enough, you would become more and more qualified for—guess what?—working for another steel pipe or industrial supply company. Sadly, your dream of a career in advertising might never be realized."

Sam pointed out, "Successful market-driven companies know precisely the direction of their business. They understand their own strengths and weaknesses and determine their own direction. The same applies if you want career success—no matter how you define *success*."

Job satisfaction and success have many definitions and can come in any size, shape, or form. Many people may reject the idea of working for a big company—nothing wrong with that, it's not for everybody.

Some may want employment at a medium size company, work for a small family business, have a degree of independence, or work at home. One just needs to decide on a direction and determine what steps are necessary to get there.

With this simple lesson, Derek understood the importance of not taking *any job* that comes along.

Despite having the notion that he could work anywhere, Derek decided to spend more time on self-analysis and researching industries and companies that fit his interests.

Derek sent Sam an e-mail:

> Dear Sam,
>
> As you said, taking any path without proper knowledge can lead to disaster. Well, I'm going to do more research and self-analysis. Hopefully, it will help me avoid *the wrong job*.

Sam replied:

> Dear Derek,
>
> Excellent! And when it comes time for your job interview, you'll be more prepared. Nine out of 10 times, interviewers will ask you to tell them about your career goals.

Chapter 5

Taking More Control of the Search

Jeff puts his mind-set in order

In Toronto, Jeff had studied pharmacology and felt that his career prospects were good. He was confident he could find something in the pharmaceutical industry. But now he wanted to find the best possible job available.

With Sam's advice, Jeff was more focused. Sam touched on five basic themes that resonated in Jeff's mind:

1. Maintain confidence
2. Be prepared
3. Choose a strategy
4. Use change to an advantage
5. Persevere

Maintain Confidence

The single most important characteristic behind successful leaders and people from all walks of life is *positive thinking*. They think in terms of success, not how to avoid failure. Professional golfer Tiger Woods is a prime example of this characteristic. He expects to win every time.

Be Prepared

U.S. Secretary of State Colin Powell said, "There are no

secrets to success. It is the result of preparation, hard work, and learning from failure." As for Tiger Woods, indeed he's a gifted athlete, but he doesn't rest on his natural abilities; he practices diligently to sharpen his skills.

Choose a Strategy

Just as in business, job hunters need to choose a strategy. Your choices are the following:

> ***Old strategy:*** Act like many failed first-generation companies by being reactive instead of proactive, just waiting for job opportunities to come your way.
>
> ***New strategy:*** Act like new generation companies of the 21st century by adopting competitive, forward-thinking, action-oriented job-hunting techniques.

Use Change to an Advantage

Jack Welch, the former chairman of **General Electric** said, "Control your destiny, or someone else will." He also said, "See change as an opportunity, not a threat."

When the business environment changes, successful companies change to meet the demand. The same applies to job hunters:

> ***Anticipate potential employers.*** Know which companies are growing. Likewise, avoid those in decline or experiencing negative factors. After all, growing companies hire more people—companies in decline don't.
>
> ***Strengthen abilities according to the market needs.*** Take courses that complement

your present abilities and teach skills that are in demand, such as logistics or marketing, to enhance your value.

Persevere

It is not uncommon for many qualified job hunters to apply at 20 or more companies and be rejected by every single one. If a similar situation occurs, persevere and determine if any modification in strategy is necessary.

Sam concluded, "I know these themes are basic. And inspiration alone won't find you a good job. But during your planning and search, your attitude will be critical to your mental condition and results."

Jeff had caught up with a friend, Doug, who had graduated in pharmacology the year before. Over coffee, they chatted about Doug's experience working at **Abbott Laboratories**. After a year on the job, Doug realized there were many career directions he could take. He could continue to do lab research work, go into marketing, or even manage a pharmacy.

Doug had seen many of his coworkers successfully make the jump to different areas of the industry. One thing stood out: Many seemed to have skills, such as marketing, to complement their degree.

After hearing Doug's story and thinking about Sam's advice, Jeff came to a conclusion. He realized that to improve his career options, he needed to enhance his skills.

Jeff sent an e-mail to Sam:

Dear Sam,

To give me some alternatives, I'm going to take

some night courses in marketing to complement my degree. During school, I realized that I didn't enjoy lab work as much as I thought I would. Maybe marketing will give me the career balance I crave.

Sam wrote back:

Dear Jeff,

You're on the right track. And maybe you'll enjoy lab work after all. But at least you'll have an alternative career choice. Best of all, most companies will love the fact that you have both lab research and marketing abilities.

Chapter 6

Many Good Jobs Are Out There—Really

Heather's first step, making choices

In Houston, Heather was anxious to make a change. But because she didn't know where to start, she was gloomy.

For the past two years, Heather worked in the marketing department of a small medical clinic. She found the job through a family friend and took it without giving it much thought.

Suffering through long hours, little pay, and bad management, Heather plainly didn't enjoy her work. Moreover, she didn't find the medical industry to be a good fit and hungered for a new career direction.

One subject Sam touched on, however, boosted her morale.

Sam said that at any given time, there are actually many more jobs available than most job hunters realize. Hundreds of companies and organizations need people all the time, but don't advertise in the classifieds or job websites and don't conduct on-campus recruiting.

Sam said that many companies just don't have the time to advertise or recruit for new staff, but nonetheless hire new people every day.

Heather thought of her friends who had found positions

at **Bank of America** and **Bechtel**, even though there were no job postings. She thought to herself, "Yeah, many people I know found jobs with companies that never posted vacancies."

Sam offered this advice: "Decide which two or three sectors you want the most, then go after them." He listed some possible sectors:

- **Government and foreign embassies.** The government needs people all the time, especially when new initiatives are started. Embassies tend to grow in line with the level of investments from their country. And there are many multilateral government organizations to consider, such as the **United Nations**, **World Bank**, **Asia Development Bank**, and **European Commission**.

- **New-generation companies.** New-generation companies with modern management skills are growing quickly from small ventures to regional or nationwide corporations.

- **Conglomerates and well-established companies.** Early generation companies still present some of the best job opportunities, and they have a wide range of business activities.

- **International companies.** Many offer a cosmopolitan environment, better pay, and localization plans to replace expatriates with local staff.

- **Small and medium size enterprises (SMEs) and start-ups.** Covering a wide variety of industries, SMEs and start-ups can carry higher risks and job instability but may offer unlimited growth.

- **Health care and education.** Working in these sectors can be highly rewarding. Certain segments are growing very fast too.

- **Foundations, nongovernment organizations (NGOs), and charities.** Such organizations offer career opportunities for those who seek to help the less fortunate or advance a cause.

- **Institutions.** Many institutions merge the secure work conditions of the government, the sharing of knowledge of the academic world, and the dynamic environment of the private sector.

Sam gave an example of one project he had worked on that hired thousands of people. It concerned a $350 million office building and a **Ritz-Carlton Hotel**. He explained that over a hundred people were hired by the project company, while thousands were hired by other companies as a result of the contracts awarded.

In-House Staff Hired	Contracts Awarded to
Engineers & Surveyors	Construction, Mechanical, Electrical, Structural, Environmental Company
Architects & Designers	Design, Interior, Lighting, Landscape Firm
Marketing & PR	Market Feasibility Consultant, Real Estate Broker, Advertising & PR Firm
Hospitality	Hotel Consultant & Operator, Spa, Food & Beverage Consultant & Operator
Finance & Accounting	Bank, Law Firm,Tax Consultant, Auditor, Insurance Broker
Administration & Secretaries	Office Supply, Equipment Leasing, IT (Information Technology) & Telecommunications Company

While some companies posted classified ads, most did not. Yet all hired many people from a wide variety of educations and backgrounds to handle this project.

If you apply this way of thinking to your targeted sector and look for segments that are active, you will see that many good jobs do indeed arise all the time.

Heather got online and wrote to Sam:

> Dear Sam,
>
> When you said that there are many more jobs available than what most people thought, I doubted you. But now I realize that many of my friends found jobs that were never posted in the classifieds.
>
> With my history major, I think I can work in just about any employment sector. I just need to prioritize two or three sectors and focus my strategy accordingly.

Sam replied:

> Dear Heather,
>
> That's the spirit. In today's global marketplace, you have so many outstanding career alternatives available to you. If you maintain your focus and carefully make choices that fit your goals, you'll definitely find many outstanding opportunities.

Chapter 7

The Typical Job Hunt—And Its Drawbacks

Carl's dose of reality, just what he needed

In Philadelphia, Carl had graduated with an accounting degree and felt he had a good chance to land a job in the accounting field. His strategy included using his university career placement center, job websites, and the newspaper classifieds.

But Carl couldn't shake a point Sam made.

Sam said that most people look for jobs by sifting through classified ads in the newspapers or job websites. Many use job fairs. Others use a network of family, friends, and contacts for help. And for fresh graduates, many seek assistance from their university career placement center.

Sam offered this parallel: "In business, if a company only looks for business opportunities in the same places where most of its competitors look, it will find success very hard to achieve."

Sam said that while using these normal channels can produce results, one should realize their drawbacks.

University Assistance

On-campus recruiting has been successful for many. Companies come to campus seeking to hire. But fresh graduates who solely use on-campus recruitment or other university assistance should realize that

- competition from fellow students will be great;
- positions offered may not be interesting;
- companies don't have time to recruit at every university in the country;
- only a small fraction of companies and organizations actually conduct on-campus recruitment;
- universities may have information for only a limited number of companies.

Some universities may have hundreds of companies that participate in on-campus recruitment. But these universities may graduate *thousands* of students each year. Clearly, not every graduate will find a job through university assistance.

Job Fairs

As job fairs typically receive wide publicity, they also attract a large number of job hunters. And often, similar to on-campus recruitment, only a limited number of companies attend. Positions offered might be limited as well.

Sam cited an example: "One job fair in San Francisco attracted 2,500 job hunters but had only 32 companies recruiting."

Attending job fairs can be worthwhile, but be aware of the great competition and limited jobs.

Classified Ads and Job Websites

Although using classified ads and job websites is one of the easiest ways to *look* for a job, bear in mind that it's one of the hardest ways to *find* success. Once a company places a job vacancy in the classifieds or on a job website, it's likely to cause a *swarm effect.* Hundreds and hundreds of people may apply for the same job. The company might also place restrictions requiring substantial experience or certain skills.

Certainly, there are many openings. But once an ad is placed, the chance of landing the job plunges.

One newspaper even pointed out that success through four top job websites averaged only 1 out of 169 because so many people apply through these popular channels. Just do the math—it's the law of chance.

Networking: Family, Friends, and Contacts

There is nothing wrong with this method. In fact, in this *it's who you know* world, it may be one of the best ways to find a job. With a good referral comes trust, a highly valued characteristic. Therefore, make use of networking whenever possible.

But understand that relying on a network to find a job also has its limitations:

- **Connections may not comprehend your objectives.** Only you fully understand your achievements, aspirations, and potential. Despite the best intentions, your connection may send you down the wrong path, with detrimental career consequences.

- **Connections may be in the wrong industry.** You may have a desire to work in one sector but your connection can only help you in an industry in which you have little or no interest.

- **Not everyone has a good network.** Many job hunters with outstanding qualifications lack such connections. Many don't belong to associations or industry groups, and many don't have great networking skills.

- **Not a sure thing.** Even with a good connection, there is no guarantee to finding a desired job. Your contact might not have enough influence over the decision-making process.

Carl met some of his friends for dinner. They had all graduated from the same university and studied accounting together, and they were all looking for jobs. They commiserated with each other about their search.

One by one, his friends would cite jobs posted in the classifieds and popular job websites. Amazingly, each had seen the same vacancy from the same source, and each had applied for the same job. Moreover, all had interviewed for jobs with the same accounting firms that recently conducted on-campus recruiting.

A disgruntled Carl thought, "Gee, all my friends are looking under the same stone for the same opportunity. Hundreds of other job hunters must be looking under the same stone too."

It was Carl's wake-up call.

Carl sent Sam a message:

Dear Sam,

Thanks for opening my eyes to some of the realities of the job search. I recognize now that I need to expand my search channels.

Sam wrote back:

> Dear Carl,
>
> Absolutely. Don't put all your eggs in one basket. Why do what everyone else is doing? Why face higher competition?
>
> Here's one more suggestion. If you're going to utilize your network, seek out contacts that might have relationships with corporate lawyers or city planners. When companies expand or invest, early in the process they usually deal with lawyers and government officials to get proper clearance. Contacts like these will know about companies that may be expanding in the near future.

Chapter 8

Casting a Wider Net: Using Multiple Channels

Ann bounces back, with focus and determination

In Los Angeles, Ann realized that Sam made a good point about the problem of choosing a job based on limited knowledge.

She unknowingly joined a company that was in poor financial condition. When its financial situation didn't improve and cutbacks were ordered, she was unfortunately chosen to be laid off. She promised herself not to make the same mistake again.

Despite being retrenched, Ann was upbeat about her chances of landing a good job. She had studied computer engineering, a discipline much in demand.

But California had been hit hard by the collapse of the Internet bubble. So Ann was also aware that the competition would be intense.

Sam said, "In life, many roads lead to the same destination." Because there are actually many channels for finding a rewarding job, job hunters should analyze which channel works best for them, perhaps focusing on the top three or four.

"Market-driven companies analyze which marketing channels work the best for them; you can act the same way too," Sam summarized.

Type of Channel	Pros	Cons
University Assistance	• Companies seek to hire • Experience not required • Companies often give training • Many good companies recruit	• Competition can be high • Companies recruit at specific times of the year • Many good companies don't recruit on-campus • Only certain jobs are offered • Not all schools attract many companies • Many universities lack a wide company database
Job Fairs	• Companies have openings • Connections are not required • Good companies attend	• Competition can be great • Only certain jobs are offered • Limited companies attend • Held only certain times of the year
Classified Ads and Job Websites	• Companies have a definite need • Job description, qualifications, contact data are provided • Openings are from many different sectors • Connections not required	• Competition can be very high • Jobs offered may not be suitable
Networking: Family, Friends, and Contacts	• Contacts may have influence over the selection process • Referral may allow easier access to the decision maker • Referral may give insights into the company that other job hunters may not have	• Company's needs are not certain • Contacts may not have enough influence • Company and job may not be interesting • No guarantees job will be offered
Employment Search Firms	• Companies have a definite need • Some firms focus on middle to upper management	• Stiff competition from experienced job hunters • Companies require an exact fit
Directly Contacting Companies	• Can decide which companies to contact • Competition from other job hunters might be lower • Decision maker might be easier to reach	• Companies may not have need • Without a referral, companies might be less interested • Must find contact information and decision maker
Temp Agencies	• Great way to gain initial experience • Can learn about companies and industries, and develop contacts • Useful way to spend time while looking for a full-time job • Many companies need temp staff • Some companies might later offer full-time employment	• Positions may not be interesting • Pay may be low • No benefits may be offered • Work contract may be for a short period

Ann wrote to Sam:

Dear Sam,

I totally agree with you. Many roads do lead to the same destination. I'm planning to focus my search efforts on temp agencies, newspaper classifieds, directly contacting companies, and using a few executive search firms.

I'm also going to improve my skills by taking some courses in Internet telephony, a segment growing very fast. With my education and experience, and complementary skills in MIS and Internet telephony, I think I can find good job offers.

Thanks also for your positive words about being laid off. I really appreciate your optimism.

Sam replied:

Dear Ann,

That's the idea! Enhancing your skills is a very wise decision.

Regarding your search, do maintain a flexible approach. Since some channels may yield more results than others, don't hesitate to adjust your strategy along the way.

And remember—being retrenched can be a blessing in disguise. You will find a job in a better company, a company that will help you boost your career. Learn from the past and avoid companies in poor condition.

Chapter 9

Be Proactive—Go Direct

Kathleen decides to "make things happen"

In Chicago, Kathleen was inspired by Sam's story of Michael Dell.

Sam said that **Dell Computer's** business model was simple—to proactively sell direct to end users, thus bypassing retail outlets that typically sell many other computer brands. Dell Computer, an idea that started out in Michael Dell's university dorm room, avoided much of the competition and became a global market leader.

"Dell made an industry," Sam said, "and is one of the great market-driven success stories in business."

Sam stated, "In job-hunting, you can avoid much of your competition by adopting a proactive market-driven strategy too. Understand that a direct approach is one of the best ways to find a job."

But Kathleen felt a little uncomfortable. She asked, "Is it OK to contact companies when they haven't advertised vacancies?"

"Kathleen, think about it," Sam said. "To maximize business opportunities, good companies don't wait for business invitations (commonly known as requests for qualifications [RFQs], requests for proposals [RFPs], and tender notices) to be advertised. They proactively seek business opportunities. It's to your benefit to act the same way.

"Also, understand that successful companies need people all the time and sometimes aren't able to place job advertisements. They may be too busy, or they delay placing the ad. They are actually pleased when someone like you, with your excellent mechanical engineering degree, contacts them."

Sam suggested thinking of it this way:

- **You'll save the company lots of money.** Placing a classified ad, hiring an executive search firm, or arranging a day of on-campus recruitment costs money. By contacting the company, you might be doing them a great favor.

- **You'll demonstrate valuable characteristics.** By directly contacting companies, your proactive approach will demonstrate that you possess some highly attractive qualities such as initiative, resourcefulness, and self-reliance.

Sam asked which alternative would be preferable:

- **To stand out more easily?** When companies don't advertise, they generally attract far fewer job applicants. Thus, if you use a direct approach, you'll have a greater chance of being noticed by the decision maker.

- **Be one of perhaps hundreds?** If you don't use a direct approach and only apply after a company advertises in the classifieds, your application could be just one of perhaps hundreds. The decision maker may not even read your application since the human resources department will likely reject all but the few short-listed applicants.

Having worked with many different types of people, Sam explained, "I understand, however, that because of your personality, being proactive and contacting companies may not be easy.

"Many people prefer to rely on connections when making contact with companies, while others choose to wait until a job opening is advertised. Well, I understand this. You can only do what you're comfortable with.

"On the other hand, you may not have the proper connections, or you may not want your life dictated by *who you know and where they work* or when companies decide to advertise for staff.

"It's your choice."

Sam also offered, "But remember what Jack Welch said: 'Control your destiny, or someone else will.'"

One day, Kathleen was surfing the web in an Internet café. She came across the website of **Unilever**, one of the top companies in the world. In the careers section about the type of employees the company looks for, she read, "people with a restless desire to make things happen."

"Of course," Kathleen thought to herself. "*Make things happen.* Successful companies like Dell and Unilever become corporate leaders because they're proactive. No doubt about it, they want proactive employees."

Kathleen sent an e-mail to Sam:

Dear Sam,

I admit that I can't stand rejection. Still, I'm going to give it a try—to be more proactive with a direct approach. As the saying goes, no risk, no reward. If Michael Dell can make things happen with a direct approach, I can too!

Sam wrote back:

Dear Kathleen,

I'll be the first to say that nobody dislikes rejection more than I. But try to look at it this way—directly contacting companies is a great way to show that you are a highly assertive person.

Realize up front, however, that not every company you contact will have a need. This is a fact of life. But by maintaining your determination you will find success. Good companies need proactive people, such as you.

And Kathleen, you can still use your network of connections too, as well as classified ads and job websites. Using several channels at the same time multiplies your chances. Remember, no single method—job search channel or interview style—works in every situation.

Chapter 10

Jobs for Every Background: Increasing Alternatives

Matt discovers more choices than he ever imagined

In Miami, Matt didn't graduate in the top tier of his interior design class; rather, he was somewhere in the middle. Because of this, he thought it would be tough to land a job at a good interior design firm.

Initially, he was pessimistic, but now he had reason to be more confident.

Sam explained two kinds of approaches to planning the job search: a conventional approach and an unconventional approach.

Conventional Approach—Limits Choices

A conventional approach limits job alternatives. Using this approach, you seek work for a company whose business is similar to your education.

For example, if you studied interior design, you might typically seek work at an interior design firm. If you studied accounting, you would look for work at an accounting firm, and so on. Many people focus on this approach with good reason, since they initially want to sharpen their skills in a company directly related to their studies, as illustrated below.

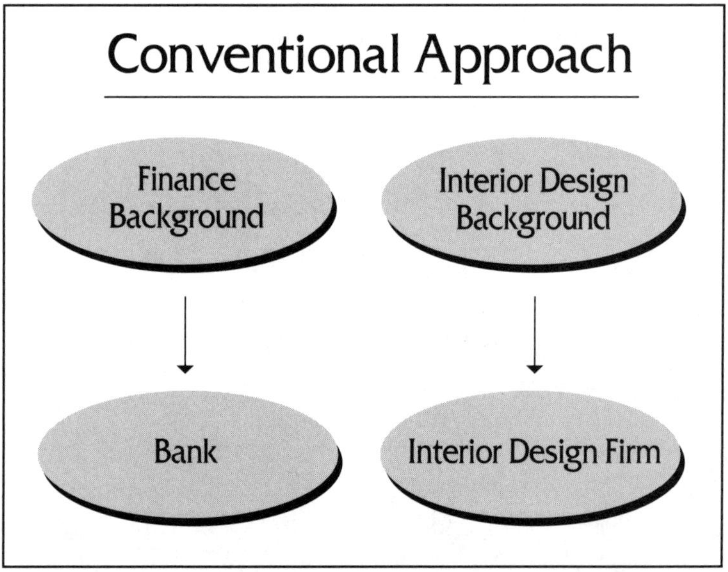

While this is common strategy with good merits, using only this approach would significantly limit Matt's job alternatives.

Unconventional Approach—Multiplies Choices

An unconventional approach can greatly improve the job search. This requires you to imagine jobs and companies that you might not have considered before. Sam referred to this as thinking *horizontally* and *vertically* in terms of job opportunities.

Consider this: You don't need to be a computer science graduate or software engineer to work for **Sun Microsystems** or **SAP**; you don't need to be a merchandising graduate or have retail experience to work for **Nike** or **Nordstrom**; and you don't need to be a finance graduate or skilled financial professional to work for **Citibank** or **Merrill Lynch**. In truth, you can be an interior design graduate, or have almost any background, and work for all of them.

Thus, besides working for an interior design firm, Matt could also find work in a bank, as shown below.

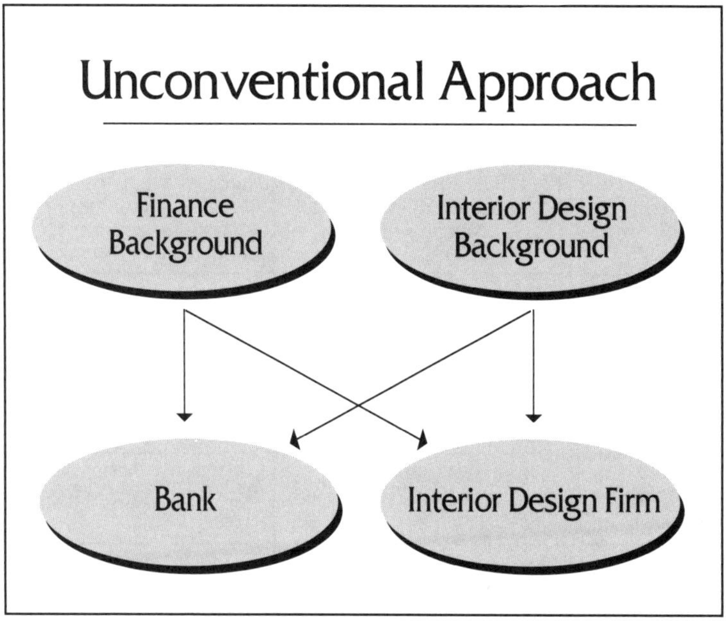

Unconventional Approach—Horizontal Strategy

To use an unconventional approach, you need to understand a little about companies. Sam said, "Realize that most medium and large companies, in sectors such as consumer products, banking, and media, need people with many different skills and education. This is thinking *horizontally* in terms of a career strategy."

He cited a typical automobile company and its various departments: "Each department has its own needs in terms of employee skills and education."

Automobile Company / Departments	Duties	Examples of Education / Experience Applicable
Production Planning and Manufacturing	Manages and plans production of vehicles	Production planning, plant and industrial management, engineering, quality control
Logistics and Procurement	Manages supply chain, warehousing, purchasing, distribution	Logistics, industrial and project management, purchasing, engineering
Product Design and Development	Develops new products and services; works with finance, production, marketing	Engineering, industrial design
Marketing, Advertising, and Public Relations	Coordinates marketing, advertising, PR, product and brand management	Management, marketing, advertising, graphics design, communications, art, PR, product and brand management
Sales and Customer Service	Coordinates sale and after-sale, dealership, call center, export and import	Marketing, brand management, international business
Finance and Accounting	Handles finance, accounting, credit risk, cash management, treasury, tax	Finance, accounting, economics, banking, investor relations, administration
Corporate and Strategic Planning	Coordinates investments, business strategies, product launch	Finance, accounting, economics, marketing, engineering
MIS, Networking, and Communications	Handles MIS, IT, data, audio, and visual communications	Computer science, IT, telecommunications, engineering
Administration and Human Resources	Manages administration, personnel, training, payroll, employee benefits, premises, facilities	Administration, HR, social science, management, corporate training, education, interior design
Legal and Public Affairs	Handles licensing, permits, copyright, tariffs, government, lawyers, community service projects	Government, law, social studies, political science, economics

As highlighted on the next page, Matt actually has several career alternatives since companies in many different industries need interior design specialists.

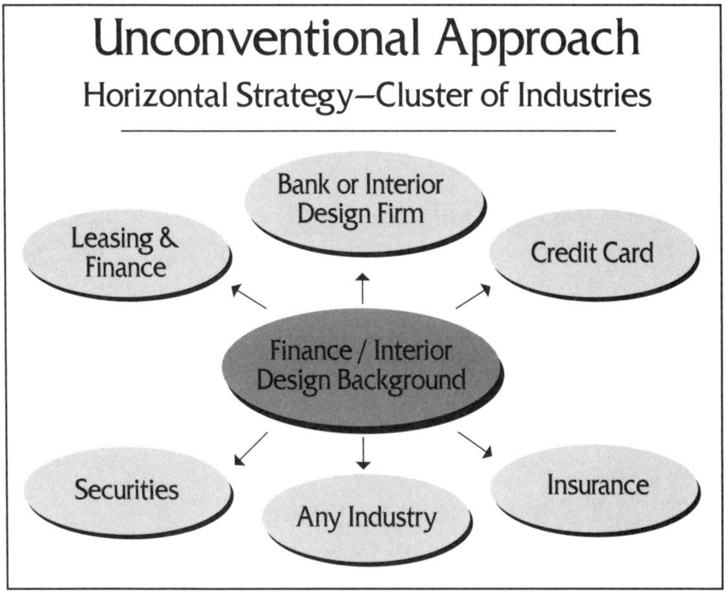
Unconventional Approach
Horizontal Strategy–Cluster of Industries
Bank or Interior Design Firm
Leasing & Finance
Credit Card
Finance / Interior Design Background
Securities
Any Industry
Insurance

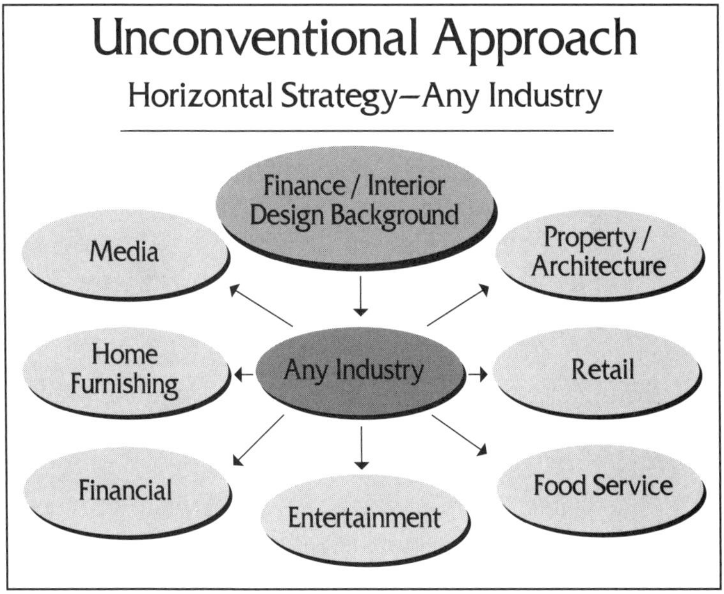
Unconventional Approach
Horizontal Strategy–Any Industry
Finance / Interior Design Background
Media
Property / Architecture
Home Furnishing
Any Industry
Retail
Financial
Entertainment
Food Service

Unconventional Approach—Vertical Strategy

Sam said that it is extremely useful to understand that every major industry is made up of different players—big, medium, and small players, equipment suppliers and contractors, and service providers and consultants—all with a focus on that particular industry.

He explained, "This applies to industries such as telecommunications, automobile, media, and entertainment. Understanding this allows you to think *vertically* in terms of a career strategy."

For example, in telecommunications, besides the major operators and handset suppliers like **Bell South** and **Nokia**, there are many other players:

Mobile and fixed line operators
Fiber optic cable services
Handset and accessory products
Internet providers
Network and switching suppliers
Broadband services
Satellite transponder services
Software consultants
Data network and consultants
Call center operations
Optical and wireless providers
Billing and customer relationship management (CRM) specialists

If the major operators are growing, other industry-related companies will likely be growing too and will probably need staff to keep up with the growth.

As illustrated on the next page, if Matt wishes to focus on the entertainment sector he would have several career alternatives available.

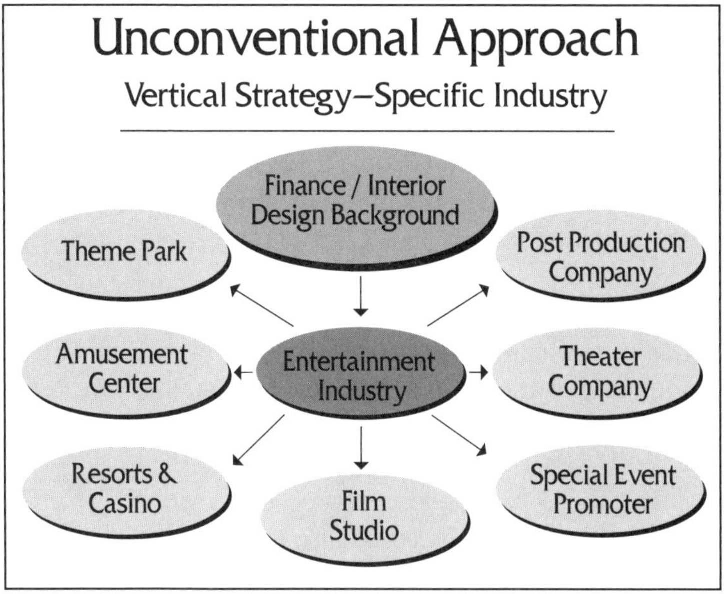

Sam said that many times, the lesser-known subindustry companies have a greater need for people, since they receive far fewer job applicants than the bigger and better-known companies.

"You could start at one of the subindustry companies, then jump to one of the bigger players after you've gained some experience," he offered.

Sam explained that he once met a bright young man from Chicago with an engineering degree who dreamed of working for a world-class auto manufacturer. He applied at major auto manufacturers such as **General Motors, DaimlerChrysler**, and **Toyota**. But he got rejected by every company and felt miserable to the point of convincing himself to stay in a company he didn't like.

Sam said, "You don't need to give up—think vertically. There are many other companies in the automobile and transportation industry that might need you, such as parts manufacturers, equipment suppliers, and distribution companies—like **Goodyear**, **Delphi**, **Johnson Controls**, and **TRW**.

"Experience at any of these companies can later make you very attractive to GM or Toyota. Just take a look at auto-related websites, like the **Automotive Body Parts Association**, to compile a list of target companies to approach."

Learning about industry players is not hard. Besides industry associations, Sam mentioned that industry magazines and trade shows are excellent sources to learn about companies.

This helped Matt realize that besides working for an interior design firm, he could also consider the entertainment industry, since he's always had a passion for music and film. But given that he has no music or film talent, he never imagined a career in entertainment.

Knowing that many industries need interior designers, he now understood that he could work for entertainment divisions of companies like **Walt Disney**, **Time Warner**, or **Sony Pictures Studio** as part of the set design team, in addition to an interior design firm.

In Matt's mind, his career alternatives had increased substantially.

He got online and wrote to Sam:

> Dear Sam,
>
> An unconventional approach has opened my eyes to many career alternatives that I never thought about before. Maybe someday soon I'll become a successful art director at a well-known film company. I'm

much more optimistic now, with something tangible and exciting to strive for.

Sam replied:

Dear Matt,

An unconventional approach is a ticket to a wonderful career. And you won't have to read about someone else having a fascinating career—you'll be living one yourself! Just don't forget me when you're rich and famous.

Part II

GET SET: PREPARATION IS THE KEY TO SUCCESS

Chapter 11

Planning the Search

Erica lays down her road map

In New York City, Erica thought a lot about Sam's planning advice, especially since she had found her first job with virtually no planning at all.

Soon after graduating, Erica got a job in a retail company through a friend. She quickly discovered that the job didn't provide the satisfaction she needed, and she wanted a change.

"You know the saying, 'Failing to prepare is preparing to fail,'" Sam offered. "If you spend time finding a job, only to realize later that the company or industry wasn't a good fit, you will have wasted valuable time, perhaps delaying your career."

Erica thought to herself, "Sam, you got that right."

Sam offered this comparison: "When a company enters a new market, it analyzes which customers to target, how to position its products, what geographical location to enter, and what price level to start at.

"If a company blindly enters a new market, it will likely encounter difficulties, if not completely fail. The same is true for job hunters.

"As Confucius said," he continued, 'The man who aims at nothing is sure to hit nothing.'"

For a job hunter, a greater chance of career satisfaction can result if a little time is invested in deciding on the sector, the industry, the companies, possible positions, and salary and location to target.

Sector

Decide which sector will be interesting and comfortable and will pave the way to your long-term objective. Consider which sector to target:

- Government
- Private
- Education or health care
- Foundations, NGOs, or charities
- Institutions

Industry

If you've chosen the private sector, decide which industries might be interesting and have good growth opportunities. Bear in mind the following:

- Condition of the industry
- Products and services offered

While considering the industry to target, ask yourself:

> **Is the industry relevant to your education, skills, and experience?** Erica has a marketing degree, so she could work in almost any industry. But certain industries, such as telecommunications and consumer products, dedicate substantially more in resources to marketing, advertising, and training than other segments.

Does the industry help build toward a long-term goal? Erica had thought about opening her own restaurant someday. Sam made her realize that she could work in the food service industry to gain valuable experience before opening her own restaurant. She could work at **Krispy Kreme** or the food and beverage department of the **Four Seasons Hotel New York**. Relevant experience will increase her chance of success when she eventually opens her own restaurant.

Can the industry satisfy certain passions? Erica is very passionate about cars and technology. She could target companies like **BMW North America** in the automotive sector or **Electronic Arts** in the computer gaming sector. No doubt about it, combining work with a personal passion is a great way to find career satisfaction—be it art, music, travel, sports, fashion, food, outdoors, science, or entertainment.

Are there many clusters of related industries or subindustries that can multiply career options? Sam had referred to this as thinking *horizontally* and *vertically*.

Companies

Once an industry is chosen, you can target a select group of companies to contact. You may decide on 10, 25, or 50 companies. In targeting companies, consider whether they are

- international or domestic;
- market leader or middle tier;
- long established or newly formed.

Sam said, "Most job hunters don't know of many companies except those most often in the media. But the market is actually filled with many excellent companies that rarely get media attention."

How would you learn about these companies? Newspapers, business periodicals, industry publications, and their websites, such as the *Seattle Times*, *San Francisco Chronicle*, *New York Times*, *Washington Post*, *Wall Street Journal*, *Fortune*, *Forbes*, and *BusinessWeek*, provide a good list of the top companies, listed and unlisted, in most major industries.

From publications such as these, you can learn about various companies, many of which have regional, national, or international operations. *Fortune*'s website, for example, has lists of companies that include the following:

Fortune 500
Global 500
America's Most Admired Companies
Global Most Admired Companies
100 Best Companies to Work For
100 Fastest-Growing Companies
100 Fastest-Growing Small Companies

It is worth noting that lists that include fast-growing small and medium size companies may present some of the best job opportunities.

Companies that have been listed in *Fortune's* 100 Best Companies to Work For and Global Most Admired Companies include well-recognized names:

100 Best to Work For	**Global Most Admired**
Cisco Systems	Nestle

Kimberly-Clark	Intel
Goldman Sachs	BMW
Alcon Laboratories	Sony
Deloitte & Touche	Nokia

Possible Positions

Deciding on possible positions is critical, as it will lay down your initial career direction. When deciding on possible positions, consider the following:

- **Self-examination.** The first step is defining *success*. What position in the future do you wish to strive for, and what job will help you get there?

  The next step is deciding on the type of job best suited for your education, abilities, goals, and personality. Are you suited for a career in marketing, sales, or research? Or are you better matched for technical, management, or administrative duties?

- **Fallback positions**. Most high achievers usually get the best jobs in the best companies. But even if you're not a high achiever, you can still find work in top companies. You might need to accept an alternative position, but the best companies are likely growing companies and will probably have needs for all kinds of people.

  Perhaps you want a career in product management in a company like **Pepsico** or **Kellogg** but find positions unavailable. Don't hesitate to inquire about possible alternative positions in call center, customer service, or distributor support operations. The experience can result in a transfer within the marketing department to a product management job—the job you may have wanted all along.

Salary and Location

A job is never finalized until the location and salary package is discussed.

Regarding compensation, it is useful to understand *the maximum you would like and the minimum you would accept*. Knowing this ahead of time will help you to negotiate with the employer.

Concerning location, you could consider your present situation as well as your future plans. Maybe you want to move from the East Coast to the West Coast, from the Midwest to the Southeast, or from the city to the suburbs. Or maybe you're forced to consider a different region of the country due to poor job market conditions in your locale. The job search should focus on companies that are expanding or have operations in those locations you desire.

Perhaps you're interested in working abroad. Consider companies that are expanding to other countries or acting as regional hubs.

Moving to another country through your career is a great way to expand your professional and cultural experience. As an expatriate, your benefits can also be greater in terms of salary, housing, transportation, and annual home leave.

Erica sent Sam an e-mail:

Dear Sam,

Planning seemed like an exhaustive task. But I have to admit, I now feel more confident and better informed about the direction of my job search.

And when I have my interviews, I'll be ready for the question, Why did you select our company for a job?

Sam wrote back:

Dear Erica,

I can't emphasize enough how right you are. With a good road map, not only will you have more confidence in your career direction, but also, from the interviewer's point of view, you'll be head and shoulders above other candidates.

How many things in life are as important as your career? Your career can be the major factor that determines your personal well-being. Thus, you owe it to yourself to plan as best as you can.

And Erica, this won't be the only time when you'll need to do this kind of planning. Throughout your life, planning, adjusting, and reinventing your career will be a constant and necessary requirement to sustain success.

Chapter 12

Assessing the Market

Wendy learns to stay ahead of the curve

In Atlanta, Wendy was in the midst of her planning. She also knew, as Sam suggested, that in addition to planning, she should assess the market.

Sam stated, "Before a market-driven company launches a new product, it conducts market analysis to determine whether there is a need for its product. The same is true for a job hunter, since, after all, you're the product that the company should want."

Sam said that this applies to all types of workers too, not just professionals. During the Internet bubble, Internet companies didn't only attract software engineers. Secretaries looking for growth opportunities found jobs in the industry too. When the industry exploded, many secretaries became millionaires from their stock options.

Thus, assessing the market can benefit every kind of job hunter.

Numerous newspapers, magazine, and websites publish industry reports. From these, a job hunter can obtain a good idea of the prevailing market conditions and business outlook in many industries, such as the following:

Growing industries. Industries that are experiencing good sales growth, have found new markets, and are investing capital to increase production will likely be looking for more staff, offering more training, and paying better salaries.

Lagging industries. Conversely, industries plagued with oversupply, financial problems, or declining demand generally hire fewer people, limit salaries, implement a hiring freeze, or retrench staff.

Subindustries. Some segments, within industries that are generally suffering, may show great promise. For example, despite the tech crash that negatively affected computer, networking, and chip companies, the gaming segment continued to do very well.

Major industries in geographical area. Some geographical areas may be heavily influenced by key industries such as hospitality, automotive, high tech, or entertainment. Following these trends will help assess the overall market condition, especially if relocation to cities such as Las Vegas, Detroit, San Jose, or Los Angeles is a consideration.

Having an idea of the economic and business trends in the industry can also benefit you during the interview. Restating factors affecting an industry and the company will demonstrate to the interviewer that you're a knowledgeable candidate.

Wendy had studied chemistry and, after graduation a year ago, found employment in a chemical supply company. Although she enjoyed her job, she found career growth opportunities slow to come in this matured industry. She wanted to make a change to a more dynamic industry.

Wendy felt that her career options could take her to any of several industries, namely oil and gas, cosmetics, pharmaceuticals and biotech, or industrial products.

Following Sam's advice about researching industries, she read in a recent issue of *Money* magazine about 10 industries that are expected to create the most new jobs over the next five years:

Advertising
Biotechnology
Cable and satellite TV
Computer software and services
Entertainment
Industrial services
Internet
Medical services
Medical supplies
Pharmaceuticals

Wendy sent Sam a message:

Dear Sam,

After doing a little research, I've decided on my career direction. I'm going to get out of the chemical industry and pursue a career in the pharmaceutical and biotech industry. This means that I'm going to target companies like **Aventis, AstraZeneca, Baxter International,** and **Biogen**.

Since this industry is growing very fast, I think I'll have a greater chance to find the career growth I need.

Sam replied:

Dear Wendy,

A little research is a wise investment. And now you

have a clearer vision why you want to pursue the pharmaceutical and biotech industry. Bravo!

But don't stop there—go to the next step. Continue to research the market to learn what positions, segments, or expertise will be in greatest demand. Perhaps a surplus of lab researchers will be projected whereas sales and marketing professionals will be in demand. Perhaps a certain segment of pharmaceuticals and biotech will be strongest, such as agriculture, nutrition, medicine, or beauty care.

That this is one of the most important facets of good career management and the job search. Having this market information and using it to your advantage will surely help you stay ahead of the hiring curve.

Chapter 13

Consider the Next Job: An Exit Strategy

Sims plans ahead, to keep options open

In Seattle, Sims, who studied communications, understood from Sam that considering the next job is important.

Sims had been working as a bank teller for two years, but he couldn't see his future in the banking industry. He felt the job wouldn't lead to anything of interest to him and that the corporate culture in banking didn't fit his personality.

Sam said that changing jobs every two or three years is common for many people, especially those in the early stages of a career. The experience gained can either catapult you to a better job or significantly hinder career growth.

Sam said, "Thinking of your next job while planning for the current job is smart. This doesn't mean you're disloyal. Rather, it's just a way to examine future alternatives and avoid dead-end possibilities. Think of this as having an *exit strategy*. It's absolutely essential for career growth."

Market-driven companies act this way all the time. Not only do they consider what initial market to enter, but they also analyze subsequent markets for future possibilities. Applying this way of thinking to your job strategy is also highly useful.

Sam reviewed a few considerations that could influence an exit strategy:

Certain industries have many thriving subindustries. The media industry is a prime example of this. Sims could work in the public relations department of a newspaper like the *Seattle Times* and later be persuaded to join a publisher like **McGraw-Hill** or a magazine such as *Cosmopolitan* with a substantially higher compensation package.

Certain industries provide critical services for other industries. The public relations industry illustrates this point very well. Sims could find a position as a communications specialist in a firm like **Hill & Knowlton** or **Ogilvy Public Relations Worldwide**. Because PR firms service many different segments, Sims might later be offered a job that advances his career in the PR department of **Micron Technology** or **Nordstrom**, or even a government agency, university, or charitable foundation.

Certain sectors might be in the twilight of its life. Remember the typewriter and pager? Sam mentioned the plight of these industries. Both were once thriving segments, with **IBM** and **Motorola** the big players. But IBM sold its typewriter division to focus on the personal computer, and Motorola successfully redirected its efforts to the mobile phone.

Sam questioned, "I wonder if employees in the typewriter and pager divisions made a similar transition to other industries? If they didn't, they'd be stuck in a dying industry with limited growth opportunities."

Nobody can say for certain which segment or product will decline next. There are always new products or services that come along to make a presently robust sector obsolete.

But keeping an eye on such trends is very useful.

Sims wrote to Sam:

> Dear Sam,
>
> As you said, some trekking paths can lead to a variety of scenic views, while other paths can lead nowhere. The same is so true in the working world—some jobs can lead to incredible alternatives, while others can lead to career stagnation.
>
> I'm planning to target the PR industry, since opportunities within and outside the industry seem so great and interesting to me.

Sam replied:

> Dear Sims,
>
> Good going. You're doing exactly what successful companies do. They plan ahead, they avoid markets in decline, and they try to maintain viable alternatives for the future.

Chapter 14

Finding Companies

Investing a little time sheds results for Sims

Still in Seattle, Sims needed to find his list of companies to contact. He recalled what Sam had talked about.

Sam knew that for many job hunters, finding names of potential employers is their biggest roadblock. But actually, finding companies is not hard at all.

He listed many sources of company information:

Telephone directories
Newspapers and trade magazines
Libraries
Stock exchanges
Foreign embassies and consulates
Chambers of commerce
Economic development agencies
Industry associations

Sam said that one shouldn't shy away from obtaining company information through these sources. If you're able to find good information, you will support the notion that you're a resourceful candidate. Companies know that resourceful people make good problem solvers.

After giving Sam's advice more thought, Sims soon discovered that there were indeed many sources of company information.

Telephone Directories

Sims learned about directories specializing in import-export, the Internet, food and beverage, advertising, financial institutions, textiles, construction and building, industrial companies, factories, and information technology.

Newspapers and Trade Magazines

Many publications have lists of top companies headquartered in their region. In Sims's regional area, the *Seattle Times* has a Northwest 100 list. On its website, the list includes companies such as **Costco Wholesale**, **Amazon.com**, **Starbucks**, and **Cray**. Sims could find company profiles and profit results, remembering that profitable companies are more likely to be hiring people.

If he ever wanted to relocate to a different region of the country, similar information could be found in other newspapers. In the *Washington Post*, its online site has The Post 200. In the *San Francisco Chronicle*, its online site has The Chronicle 200.

In the vicinity of Washington, D.C., Sims could learn about companies such as **Marriott International**, **Mars**, **Geico**, and **Discovery Communications**. In the San Francisco area, he could learn about companies such as **ChevronTexaco**, **NVIDIA**, **PMC-Sierra**, and **Pixar**. Though many of these companies might never recruit in Seattle or at Sims's college in Oregon, he could now contact them directly.

Libraries

Besides public and university libraries, there are other libraries in the private sector. Many major newspapers maintain libraries that are open for public use. And the library at the **Japan External Trade Organization (JETRO)** has tons of information about companies, especially those from Japan.

Stock Exchanges

Many major and regional stock exchanges, such as the **New York Stock Exchange**, **NASDAQ**, and **Pacific Stock Exchange**, maintain libraries, resources centers, and websites useful to the public. These centers are filled with company information and industry reports.

Foreign Embassies and Consulates

Foreign embassies and consulates normally maintain a library in their commercial section, which is usually open to the public. Also, when a foreign company opens a new office, they typically visit their diplomatic mission to meet people and learn about local laws. As a result, commercial sections might be able to inform you of companies making investments that may need new staff.

In Seattle, Sims learned that there were consulates from New Zealand, Canada, and the United Kingdom, as well as JETRO in nearby Vancouver. Sam said that these are great places for company information that few job hunters consider.

Chambers of Commerce

Many domestic and international chambers and business organizations maintain directories of members, which include contact information and company profiles.

Sims soon learned about the **British American Chamber of Commerce** in Seattle, which has information for U.K. companies such as **Rolls Royce** and **BAE Systems**.

Economic Development Agencies

Such organizations spearhead government efforts to

promote business and investment to their region. On their websites, they often provide useful data, such as regional chambers of commerce, new investments by companies, and other sources of business information.

Sims discovered that the websites of the **Economic Development Council of Seattle & King County** and the **Office of Economic Development** contain a wealth of information.

Industry Associations

National and regional associations can have memberships that total hundreds of companies, all of which conduct business within a specific industry. In public relations and advertising, Sims discovered excellent information on the websites of the **Public Relations Society of America** and the **American Association of Advertising Agencies**.

On the Washington Secretary of State website, Sims found a directory of associations, which includes the **Association for Information and Image Management, Washington Software Alliance, Washington Association of Wine Grape Growers, and Washington Association of Accountants**. Through these websites or a quick trip to their offices, Sims would be able to learn about many companies.

Sims wrote to Sam again:

> Dear Sam,
>
> Following your advice, I discovered many companies in my chosen field of interest—public relations. And not just PR firms but also companies that have a communications and PR department, within and outside the Seattle area.

Sam wrote back:

> Dear Sims,
>
> I know it required effort on your part. But investing a little time can produce results. Plus you're showing excellent signs of being a highly self-reliant person. Not only will good companies be pleased to interview you, but also you'll have more job alternatives available, putting you in the driver's seat.

Chapter 15

Jobs Abroad

Carl's search, half a world away

In Philadelphia, Carl is reminded every day of the competitive employment market. Because markets abroad may be better, he has decided to look for a job in China. But how?

He has no family and only a few contacts in China. But with the economy booming and his ability to speak Chinese, he felt there had to be better opportunities abroad.

As Sam suggested, good planning and focus is key. With this view, Carl decided to focus on two industries that were especially bright in China—automotive and telecommunications.

Using Sam's guidance, Carl began to compile information about companies in his targeted industries. He used industry associations, chambers of commerce, embassies, and other online sources from China. He also followed industry trends daily by browsing websites of newspapers such as Hong Kong's *South China Morning Post* and the *Shanghai Daily*.

Carl soon learned that these companies were expanding operations:

Automotive	**Telecommunications**
GM China	Nortel Networks (China)
BMW	Ericsson (China)
DaimlerChrysler	China Unicom
Nissan	Alcatel (China)
FAW-Volkswagen	Motorola (China)
Toyota China	Nokia (China)
Beijing Automotive-Chrysler	Siemens
Shanghai Volkswagen	NTT DoCoMo
AC Delco	Huawei Technologies
Delphi Automotive Systems	China Telecom

Sam also conveyed that jobs abroad originate in many different locations. He said that while you can look overseas for jobs, one shouldn't hesitate to contact regional or head offices. Companies with international operations, such as **Coca-Cola** and **Oracle**, constantly send employees abroad from their headquarters.

To address whether or not speaking a foreign language is necessary, Sam offered some useful insights. Sam mentioned that while working overseas he had met several expatriates from America, Australia, and Great Britain who were posted in countries like Japan, China, and France. Yet most of these expats had little foreign language talent. What stood out, however, was their solid experience and professional abilities.

Thus, is speaking a foreign language really a necessity? Generally yes—if you're an entry-level applicant with little experience. But likely no—if you're an experienced professional with outstanding qualifications. Is speaking a foreign language a benefit for a seasoned professional? Absolutely.

Sam said he worked in places like Japan, China, and Germany. Could he fluently speak the language of his host country? No.

Carl sent Sam an e-mail:

> Dear Sam,
>
> With your suggestions, I've already found a good list of companies to contact in China. Soon I'm going to make a trip abroad to explore further.

Sam replied:

> Dear Carl,
>
> Provided you're mobile, relocating to a stronger job market is a good idea. And take note—you can also contact the North American offices of companies expanding in China as a starting point.
>
> Additionally, realize that smaller companies are expanding internationally too. So your search does not need to be limited only to big multinationals. Many small and medium size companies may be interested in investing in China. You can always contact their head offices.
>
> Working abroad is an unattainable dream for many people. Actually, finding work abroad is not that hard. You just have to try. And it all starts with a good list of potential employers, which you now have. Dream jobs are attainable.

Carl wrote back to Sam:

> Dear Sam,
>
> I can't thank you enough for your advice! I was in touch with a college friend who lives in Iowa and got a great tip. He read in the *Des Moines Register* that **Principal Financial Group** from Des

Moines was exploring the possibility of investing in China. It has investments in Mexico and Chile, and is looking at India as well. I'm going to quickly contact this company with the hope of helping them enter the China market.

Chapter 16

Read the News: Job Opportunities Every Day

Go-Getters in the news

In Miami, Kansas City, Houston, Chicago, Los Angeles, and Philadelphia, Matt, Derek, Heather, Kathleen, Ann, and Carl hadn't yet found success.

But they were reminded of Sam's advice. He said, "Don't hesitate to complement your search by keeping a lookout for hints of other job openings. Newspapers, magazines, and trade publications are a great source for this. And I'm not just talking about the classified section."

Sam said that it's easy to be one step ahead of most job hunters. When most job hunters look in newspapers they usually turn to the classified section. Sam suggested to first look at the business, finance, real estate, automotive, and technology sections.

Sam summarized, "Companies look for business opportunities all the time in the newspapers. For example, if a construction company learns from the property section of a newspaper that a new hotel project is being planned, you can be sure that its marketing officer will soon contact the hotel developer for construction opportunities.

"As a job hunter, you can act the same way and also contact the hotel developer," Sam said. "You're just not selling construction services; you're selling yourself, since the developer will surely need to assemble a project team.

"There are hints of job openings in these sections every day," Sam claimed. "And this is well before companies place job vacancy ads in the classifieds.

"Take note of buzzwords like *expansion and development plans, increasing investments, rising capital expenditures (or capex), higher R&D spending, new markets,* and *improving sales and profits*. These can mean solid hints of a company's brighter employment picture."

Sam reviewed typical sources of such information:

Daily newspapers	News websites
Business newspapers	Business websites
Business magazines	Industry trade magazines

He especially highlighted industry trade publications, since they usually contain a tremendous amount of up-to-date information about a particular industry that may be of interest to a job hunter.

Sam cited different kinds of articles to look for:

News of the establishment of a new company, office, or regional headquarters. When a company establishes a new presence, it generally needs new staff as well. If it opens a regional headquarters, national or international work could be available.

News of new projects or expansion. A new hotel project, power plant, or factory requires many entry-level and experienced people, during construction and upon completion. The ramp-up stage, when many people are initially hired, usually starts several months before construction starts.

News of new products or services. Managing new products and services at times requires a new division or expansion of an existing department. With this, there may be a need for staff of all kinds in marketing, product management, and administration.

News of a new corporate strategy. A company may enter a new industry, a new segment, or may venture overseas. Whatever the case may be, a new corporate strategy can mean job openings.

News of a new contract signed. Just as signing a new contract is good for a company, it is also good for a job hunter. Implementing a contract requires a planning and ramp-up stage as well as a full execution stage, where new people are required at each different phase.

News of an outsourcing deal. One of the biggest trends in business today is outsourcing. A company taking on such a contract could be an accounting firm, payroll specialist, IT company, logistics company, or manufacturing company.

News of a joint venture, merger, or acquisition. When such a transaction is concluded, it could mean that additional cash may be injected into the company, with a large portion earmarked for business expansion. Some deals, however, can mean job cuts.

News of a financing deal. Follow the money, and you'll find jobs. Anytime a company raises money through an initial public offering (IPO), bond deal, debenture, syndicated loan, venture capital investment, or private placement, it will have plans to use the funds. These plans may include expanding the business, building a new factory, improving the product line, or developing new projects.

News of improved business activity or financial results. When sales and profits grow, companies are normally more optimistic about the future and will be in better positions to hire more people.

News of stock price run-up. A company's stock price to a large degree is based on expectation. If the stock price has been increasing, it could mean that the company's business outlook is bright.

Profiles of companies or executives. A profile of a company or executive can reveal good job leads. It is common in such articles to include news of new products, overseas expansion, newly signed contracts, financing deals, or new strategies.

News of new franchises. Franchises could involve restaurants, beauty shops, learning centers, and product representatives.

News of government approvals, licensing, or patents. When a company wins FDA approval of a drug, FAA approval of an airline route, or patent approval of an invention, it could be an indication of greater business activity to come.

Announcements of management appointments or promotions. When a new manager takes charge of a department, new initiatives may start to take the company to new markets, or a higher level of production, or to solve problems. New staff is often required.

News of regional development and economic activities. Government and private organizations promote business, relocation, and investment in their area. Often their websites contain useful news of new companies that are expanding.

News of government initiatives. Articles about national, state, provincial, or municipal government initiatives can give an idea which departments to focus attention on. Even mundane budget information can be useful, since departments with bigger budgets will likely increase their head count.

News of foundation fundraising. When an education institute or a non-profit organization is awarded a grant, or if a charitable foundation increases its grant programs, such activity could mean unique job opportunities in this sector.

Sam said, "If you see any of these articles, don't be surprised if you see a job posting a few weeks or months later. In many cases, you might never see a classified ad. So why wait to contact the company? If you do, you'll only face more competition.

"Throughout my career, I've been involved in many new projects, financing arrangements, awarding of contracts, joint ventures, and corporate expansion plans that resulted in the hiring of thousands of people. I helped plan the ramp-up process and hiring schedule. I hired lawyers to obtain government permits. And I helped draft press releases announcing new initiatives for the media and gave approval to the HR department to list job vacancies in the classifieds and on the Internet a few months later.

"Move quickly on these leads," Sam advised.

He continued, "Other hints of jobs can also be found in newspaper listings of RFQs, RFPs, and tender notices. These notifications generally mean that companies are calling for bids on project or procurement opportunities. For a job hunter, it could mean that these companies might be in an expansion mode.

"Leads can also be uncovered in press releases posted on company websites. Press releases often cite business expansion or new projects."

In **Miami**, Matt read in *Amusement Today* magazine that **Cedar Fair**, the owner of Knott's Berry Farm and other theme parks, will invest $25 million on new rides and expansion. He also read in *Amusement Business* magazine that **Paramount Parks** has started to design a $1 billion 123-acre movie-based theme park in Japan.

Matt felt that with such activity, both companies might need good interior designers.

In **Kansas City**, Derek noted in the *St. Louis Post-Dispatch* that Kansas City-based **DST Systems** will open a $50 million data center in Bridgeton by the end of this year.

Derek thought, "Surely, with this project the company might be looking for people."

In **Houston**, Heather read in the *Houston Chronicle* that the real estate market has been very active.

She reasoned that top real estate developers, such as

Clayton Homes and **Centex Homes**, might be more inclined to hire additional staff.

In **Chicago**, Kathleen read on the website of *Development* magazine that **Higgins Development Partners** and **Pritzker Realty Group** announced the groundbreaking of Hyatt Center, a 1.7 million-square-foot development in Chicago.

Kathleen understood from Sam that for a project like this, the developer, main contractor, and subcontractors would likely need mechanical engineers.

In **Los Angeles**, Ann read in the *San Francisco Chronicle* that **Dolby Laboratories** is planning a $100 million IPO and that the company is rapidly expanding. The article stated that Dolby's workforce is growing, that 20 job openings are available, and that the company recently hired a PR director and an in-house lawyer.

"Wow," Ann said to herself, "Sam's right. Companies that raise money do indeed hire many people."

She also read on the website of the *San Jose Mercury News* that several Bay Area companies recently raised venture capital funds, including **CoTherix** and **Threshold Pharmaceuticals**, indicating possible job openings.

In **Philadelphia**, Carl read in *Reuters* that **Volkswagen** and **First Automotive Works** will double capacity with a $1.15 billion investment in Changchun, China. The article also reported that **General Motors** is investing $240 million to expand its Shanghai facility, and that **Nissan Motors** announced a $2 billion venture with **Dongfeng Motors** to build vehicles in China.

He also read in the *Asian Wall Street Journal* that **China Netcom** plans to issue 5 billion yuan (about $600 million) of corporate bonds to finance network expansion.

Carl thought this news definitely would mean job openings in China for these companies.

They all wrote to Sam updating their progress.

Sam wrote back:

> Dear All,
>
> Good work. I'd say you're all acting in a savvy market-driven way. And I completely agree—don't wait until these companies advertise in the classifieds to contact them. Contact these companies soon after news of their expansion activities is announced, well before they post job openings, well before your competition finds out.
>
> And if you have friends in college, be sure to tell them that they can find internships and part time jobs using this same strategy. After all, companies that are expanding are more likely to provide opportunities for college students compared to companies in decline. And just maybe, the internship or part-time work will turn into a full-time job after graduation.
>
> Given the difficult job market over the past several years, students in college today would be smart to consider this strategy before graduation to gain valuable experience and possibly arrange a full-time job.

Chapter 17

Industry Trade Shows: Shopping Mall for Job Hunters

Ann finds leads and contacts everywhere

In Los Angeles, Ann especially noted Sam's comment about industry exhibitions, as Southern California is one of the top exhibition locales in the country.

Sam pointed out that companies attend trade shows to promote their business. They use these venues to showcase their existing business as well as newly launched products, projects in the planning stage, and services soon to be offered. Companies also attend to seek business opportunities.

Trade shows can be a shopping mall for a job hunter. They are wonderful venues to collect solid job leads.

Even if you're uncertain about the industry as a career path, attending industry trade shows can be an excellent way to gain knowledge about whether to pursue the industry.

Sam had these suggestions:

Look for new projects. Many companies use trade shows to present their strategies and announce favorable news. For example, you might find hints of job opportunities such as these:

- **North America Forest Products Conference** (San Diego). Perhaps companies like **Georgia-Pacific** or **Owens-Illinois** will announce an IT initiative to streamline its logistics and distribution that will start in six months.

- **Chem Show** (New York City). Perhaps companies such as **Shell** and **Dow Chemical** will display a model of their new petrochemical plant to come online in 18 months.

- **Biomakers in Drug Discovery** (Boston). Maybe a leading biotech company such as **Genentech** or **Amgen** will announce a new discovery or government approval that will pave the way for wide manufacturing and distribution.

New projects and expansion activities definitely indicate the possibility of job opportunities.

Make valuable contacts. Trade shows provide for excellent networking opportunities. Take the initiative to talk to company representatives, show interest in the company, and gather name cards. You can follow up later. But be careful not to seek a job too overtly. Representatives do not attend these trade show to recruit new staff.

Work part time. Many exhibitors hire temporary staff to hand out brochures and carry out minor duties. Working part time is a wonderful way to meet people in the company or industry of your interest.

Learn about exhibitors. Learning about upcoming exhibitions, names of participants, and event organizers in advance can be done by searching the web for convention and visitor bureaus, exhibition venues, and exhibition planners. You can also check the newspapers for a calendar of events schedule.

Ann sent Sam a message:

Dear Sam,

I've already attended a few IT shows and have learned about other upcoming exhibitions in the Los Angeles and San Diego areas.

Exhibitions are great places to learn about new projects and make contacts. So far I've found hints of job opportunities everywhere!

Sam replied:

Dear Ann,

Excellent. And remember, if you check the websites of these exhibitions in advance, many times they provide names of the major companies that attend as exhibitors. You could easily contact a company or the exhibition planner and apply for a part-time job. It's a great way to make contacts with a company you're interested in.

Part III

GO: TURNING DREAMS INTO REALITY

Chapter 18

Making Contact Requires a Little Digging and Finesse

Erica and the art of contacting companies

In New York City, Erica was anxious to pursue some leads. But she was at a roadblock.

Though she had found some interesting prospects in the business section of newspapers, she didn't have their contact information. She then recalled some of Sam's tips.

Finding Companies

Sam felt that getting in touch with a company listed in the classified ads was easy. All the contact information is provided.

But if you want to contact a company that you've just read about in the newspaper, it takes a little effort. But it isn't difficult either.

Sam understood that exact names and contact information of companies are rarely reported in the newspaper. Moreover, during a start-up phase, companies often occupy temporary offices, offices of a customer, or makeshift project offices, and aren't yet listed in local telephone directories.

He said not to be discouraged, and reviewed a scenario on how to find a company's contact information: Let's say you read a newspaper article about a British company that has just opened an office in New York City. The report says the company is planning to expand its business in the New England area first, with expected expansion nationwide. But all you know is the name of the company and that it's from the United Kingdom. Here's how to find the New York City office contact information:

1. Look in the telephone book → NYC office contact
2. Call the telephone operator → NYC office contact
3. Call the British Consulate in NYC → commercial section → NYC office contact
4. Call the British Business Council → NYC office contact
5. Call a related industry association → NYC office contact
6. Search for the company's U.S. website → NYC office contact
7. Search for the company's U.K. website → global locations → NYC or regional office contact
8. Send an e-mail to the head office in U.K. → NYC office contact

Finding any company is as simple as that.

If the company you're looking for is a domestic company from another region of the country, a similar procedure can be followed.

Sam added, "If asked during an interview, How did you find our company? you will have a good answer to highlight your resourceful skills.

"Additionally, if finding the company took some effort, consider this a positive, since you'll likely encounter less competition from other job hunters."

The Decision Maker vs. The Human Resources Department

Once you have the contact information, you're then ready to approach the company. Before you start, it's useful to understand the role of the human resources department.

Sam said that the HR department performs a job applicant filter role for the departments it supports. As a job hunter, your goal is to be short-listed above the other job applicants or to completely bypass the HR department and correspond directly with the decision maker.

Sam said that many successful job hunters choose the latter strategy. It saves time, reduces the chance of being rejected by the HR department, and sets you apart from other job applicants.

However, the HR department can be very influential. Give this department the respect it deserves, because the decision maker might instruct you to first contact the HR department.

Sam mentioned something of special value to Erica. He said, "Erica, you studied marketing. If you get a marketing job, you'll be expected to reach the decision maker to sell your product. Most bosses won't care what channels you use, only the results."

He added, "During your job search, if you directly pursue the decision maker, you may stand a better chance of showing that you're a results-oriented person.

"Even if you're instructed to send your application to the HR department, there's no rule against you sending a duplicate correspondence to the decision maker. In fact, it might be a good way to get noticed."

Erica understood Sam's point very well.

Understanding Conglomerates and Large Companies

Conglomerates and large companies usually have many different business units in different industries. Understanding this can make a huge difference in your career.

Many people join large successful companies but end up in business units they have little interest in. If internal transfers are not possible, they may eventually leave the company.

Had they carefully chosen the right business unit to target, their career might be entirely different.

Sam cited **General Electric** as a prime example.

Erica took note of this and located GE's website, which contained information about several different business units. "Absolutely," she thought. She found GE involved in the following:

Adhesives and sealants
Appliances
Automotive
Aviation
Business finance
Business products
Consumer electronics
Energy
Health care
Home comfort and safety
Insurance
Lighting
Personal finance
Protection plans
Retail
Television media
Transportation

With this information, before Erica contacts GE, she can at least think about the business unit to target in advance.

If Erica has no preference, she could even apply at several of the business units, since each might have its own hiring process, thus multiplying her chances of working for a great organization like GE.

Approaching the Appropriate Decision Maker

Erica wasn't sure who would be the appropriate contact. With little work experience, she wasn't familiar with corporate structure.

But she welcomed her mentor's guidance. Sam explained that depending on the position and department targeted, the decision maker could be any one of several people:

Managing director	Department manager
General manager	Section manager
Division director	Office manager
Project manager	Section supervisor
Operations manager	Senior secretary

Sam continued, "Normally, the key decision to hire you comes from the person who will eventually supervise you. If you're seeking an entry-level position, your boss might be the department manager, section manager, office manager, or section supervisor. Your application should be directed to that person."

He reviewed a possible scenario:

> Perhaps you've decided to apply for an entry-level position in the marketing and sales department of a company.

1. Gather information from the HR department. Explain that you want to know about possible sections and positions in the sales and marketing department, such as corporate sales, telemarketing, sales support, competitive research, advertising, public relations, and customer service. Seek information concerning

    - Possible entry-level marketing positions

- Job opportunities in expanding sections
- New departments under development

2. Learn about the decision maker. You can contact the receptionist or administrative assistant in the marketing department and focus your inquiry on the section you're interested in. Obtain the

    - Section manager's name and title
    - Office address
    - Name of department
    - Telephone number and fax number
    - Administrative assistant's name

3. Mail a hard copy of your cover letter and resume to the decision maker. If you send your application by e-mail, seek help from the decision maker's assistant. Request help to

    - Receive your e-mail and attachments
    - Provide a hard copy of your cover letter and resume to the decision maker

    Striking up a friendly and polite relationship greatly helps. You need to obtain the assistant's e-mail address in this case.

Sam said that decision makers are usually very busy people. Many managers return from business trips with loads of e-mail messages in their in-box. If you send your application directly to the decision maker, your e-mail might go unread. It's just a reality of the working world.

But with the help of an assistant, there might be a better chance that your application will be reviewed, since it will be sitting right on the manager's desk *waiting to be read.*

Sam said, "Now you can see the difference between two strategies—using a direct approach and using classified ads, job websites, and job fairs.

"By using a direct approach, you choose when to apply and which company, which business unit, and which department you wish to apply to.

"Those who only use classified ads, job websites, and job fairs *wait* until the opportunity arises and *hope* the company, business unit, and department are to their liking."

He continued, "And think of it this way. In business, market-driven companies don't blindly send business proposals to prospective customers. They properly research who the proposal should be sent to, and they send the proposal directly to the decision maker. As a job hunter, the same applies to you."

Sam concluded, "Finally, this is where your tenacity and resolve to succeed will be tested. You may not obtain the necessary information in one telephone call. You may need to call back a few times. Don't give up.

"Once you have the necessary information, you'll at least feel that you have a shot."

Erica wrote to Sam:

> Dear Sam,
>
> Your suggestions on approaching companies have been extremely beneficial. Your inside tips, invaluable!

Sam wrote back:

Dear Erica,

And don't forget—once you start working, you'll be approaching other companies all the time. Thus, approaching prospective employers intelligently shows that you are professional and results-oriented.

I realize that I've given you several different guides concerning the job search, career planning, finding companies, and approaching employers. Understand that these guides won't apply to everyone or every situation. Use only what works best for you.

Chapter 19

Follow-Up: Success for Those Who Don't Give Up

Derek decides, "I really want this job"

In Toronto, despite sending out more than 20 resumes, Jeff received a reply from only one company. He knew he had to follow up.

Sam said that follow-up is absolutely critical in the job search. He commented, "It's amazing that so many people don't bother to follow up."

Many job hunters feel that if the company doesn't contact them, they're not wanted. People automatically assume that they've been rejected, so they don't follow up, perhaps afraid of being rejected again.

Sam explained, "In business, companies know that following up on proposals is essential. They know that the chance of success increases with effective follow-up."

Reasons for Following Up

Sam said that perhaps companies have indeed rejected you. But consider the following:

- **Managers are too busy to contact you or haven't read your resume yet.** Take this as a positive sign that the department is very busy and may need additional staff. A follow-up call is the only way to assess this.

- **Managers may be undecided about your qualifications.** They may not have rejected you outright. They just might not be 100 percent convinced they should interview you. Making a follow-up call could nudge the company in your favor.

- **Managers are not sure what position is best for you.** A follow-up call would allow you to explain how you could benefit the department. This is where selling yourself is necessary.

- **Managers may want to test you.** Managers sometimes test applicants before taking the time for an interview. They want to see if applicants possess characteristics that would make them productive employees. They see follow-up as a sign of persistence, maturity, and courage—all necessary traits to succeed in the working world.

- **Managers may not have an immediate need, but might later.** Most successful companies have new projects, new products to launch, or new expansion plans in the pipeline. A follow-up call may not land an immediate interview, but it might give insights to contact the company at a later date. Plus, the decision maker will already know you. So don't hesitate to ask about future possibilities.

The Follow-Up Call

Before making the follow-up call, Sam suggested thinking of the following possible responses to the scenarios described above. You'll be better prepared.

1. **Recognize the best time to make the call.** Managers are most busy from 9 A.M. to 12 noon and 2 P.M. to 4 P.M. They have to attend to meetings, appointments, and other matters. If you call later in the day, perhaps between 4 P.M. and 6 P.M., you might reach the decision maker at a less busy time when you could have a more relaxed and productive conversation.

2. **Be ready to sell yourself.** Sell yourself in a clear, concise, and organized manner. If the situation requires, be ready to cite an example from your past experience or education. If the need isn't made clear, don't hesitate to turn the tables. Sam suggested asking, "What type of person do you need?" Be ready to answer how you're that type of person.

3. **Once the manager agrees to explore further, ask to schedule an interview.** Make yourself available for the interview dates convenient to the manager.

In his experience, Sam was always impressed with those who followed up. He valued their determination and persistence, and respected their spirit to face rejection. Sam reasoned, "Those who follow up effectively during the job search indicate that they can do the same if hired."

Sam concluded, "The bottom line is this: *Just how much do you want the job?*"

Jeff got online and sent Sam a message:

> Dear Sam,
>
> I have to admit, I was not too keen to follow up. But you gave me good reasons why it's to my benefit. Even if only one or two companies agree to meet me, that's better than none.

Sam replied:

> Dear Jeff,
>
> That's the attitude. Remember, follow-up doesn't end by simply sending a thank you note. It is all about effectively getting to the next step—whether it concerns getting the initial interview, getting a second interview, or getting the job offer after the final interview.
>
> Follow-up will definitely distinguish you over many other candidates. Keep it up.

Chapter 20

The Interview: Know Yourself Well

Wendy prepares, with confidence

In Atlanta, Wendy was ready for her interviews. She was nervous. But she found Sam's advice helpful.

Sam said that he had interviewed countless numbers of people.

"After so many interviews, I could distinguish the canned answers from the thoughtful and genuine responses. Certainly, I appreciated the latter, since I felt I was learning more about the person," he said.

Sam knew that there was no shortage of books on how to interview and that some provided good suggestions. But in some instances, he felt some candidates relied on them too much.

Wendy recalled many of her friends who had read these books and memorized answer after answer. They filled their minds with details to get ready for possible *what if* questions. But during the interviews, they were never asked the questions they had prepared for. And what's more, because they had tried to memorize so many answers they tripped over some of the easier questions.

Sam conveyed, "It is extremely difficult to predict and prepare for *what if* questions. While some interviewers certainly do inject such questions during the interview, most interviewers are generally very straightforward."

Sam offered, "The best advice I can give you is to keep it simple—be natural and know yourself well." He felt it was particularly important to know

- why you studied at your university and why you chose your particular major;
- why you worked for your previous employer and why you want to change jobs;
- why you contacted this company and why you selected this industry;
- why you think you can do a good job and why you're a good candidate;
- the positives of your character, your set of skills, and how they can help you at work;
- how you work smoothly in an organization;
- the chief accomplishments and challenges in your life and what you did to achieve results and overcome obstacles;
- your added-value abilities and how they can help the company;
- your employment conditions;
- the potential career path you envision.

"If you know yourself well," Sam stated, "you should be able to handle most interviews without problems, including most *what if* questions should they arise."

Sam also felt that answers should show a purpose. He suggested avoiding such answers as "I studied at my university because my brother studied there" or "I found your company because my friend works here."

Rather, have a good purposeful answer such as "The university was known to have a good chemistry department" or "Your company is one of the top companies in the pharmaceuticals industry with impressive research and development." Have supporting information in mind to back up these statements, just in case.

He offered some additional advice:

- **Internship experience.** Detail what you learned about the company and the industry, but also be prepared to answer why you're not working for that company. For many, an internship is also a way to learn about a company or industry that isn't a good fit.

- **Brochures, drawings, photos, or reports.** Presenting materials related to your previous experience or accomplishments can underscore your abilities and enhance the positive perception that you're a person who comes to an important event prepared.

- **Research the company and industry.** Obviously, knowing important factors about the company and industry is important. But generally it's not necessary to memorize detailed facts. Just have an overall picture of relevant matters.

- **Clear, concise, and organized responses.** There is no such thing as *the best answer*. But your answers should be clear, to the point, and well organized.

- **Answer the question.** Avoid *dancing around the question*, since it will leave a negative impression.

- **Avoid simple yes or no answers.** Providing supporting information is essential.

- **Ask questions pertinent to the interview and position you seek.** By asking good questions, you can demonstrate that you can digest information during the conversation and recognize where clarification is needed, whether it is about the company, job description, growth opportunities, or performance expectations.

"I know an interview has many different components," Sam claimed. "All job hunters go to great lengths to prepare for them—in terms of personal appearance, verbal abilities, body language, likeable personality, education, job skills, and experience. This is fine. But never forget the overriding business objective of the interview *from the company's standpoint.*

"The bottom line for companies is that they want to know if you have the capabilities to increase business, lower costs, solve problems, increase efficiency, reduce risks, create something, or effectively manage a given situation. When the opportunity arises, be sure that your answer reflects how you could help the company achieve any of these goals.

"This same logic applies if you're already employed and wish to convince your boss that you can handle a new responsibility or an advancement in your career."

Wendy e-mailed Sam:

Dear Sam,

Thanks for introducing some real-world insights

about the interview process. I feel more relaxed and confident now. And I'm going to bring to the interviews my research paper on the pharmaceutical industry.

Sam wrote back:

Dear Wendy,

I know you'll do great. And bringing your research paper is an excellent idea. But to keep your presentation concise, you might want to prepare an executive summary of your paper. Presenting an executive summary will surely be impressive.

Chapter 21

What Companies Look For

A good story, a great interview

Each of the Go-Getters had lined up several interviews. Using Sam's advice, they had each received interest from a number of their targeted companies. They were cautious but optimistic.

This was their final hurdle.

Sam's final counsel was now on their minds. Over the years, he had interviewed many people for different companies, both U.S. multinationals and international conglomerates. They felt confident with his advice.

Sam explained that companies certainly check to see if your education and/or experience complement the job requirement. But equally important, successful and progressive companies look for certain qualities in your character:

- **Education.** There should be a good fit, especially for entry-level positions.

- **Work experience.** While many companies claim that work experience is not required for entry-level jobs, if you've got the right experience you will definitely have an advantage. For middle- and upper-level jobs, related experience or transferable skills would definitely be a factor.

- **Good attitude and potential to grow.** Companies

see these fundamental qualities as essential for an employee to succeed and take on more responsibilities.

Sam had learned that while ability can help you succeed, character is what keeps you there.

"Character," he said, "is what companies look for in candidates to complement education and experience."

Sam listed several characteristics that underscore a good attitude and potential to grow:

Adaptable to change	Integrity
Alertness	Learns from mistakes
Creativity	Poise under pressure
Confidence	Proactive behavior
Drive	Responsibility
Enthusiasm to learn	Self-disciplined
Focus	Self-reliant
Good communications	Sound logical thinking
Industrious	Team spirit

How do companies learn if candidates possess such characteristics? Today, many companies use situational, behavioral, or case study interviews. Companies feel that these types of interviews predict performance much better than a standard interview.

In one survey, situational interviews were shown to substantially exceed standard interviews in terms of predicting performance.

Such interviews provide a glimpse at how candidates act in a given situation or how they

- display opportunistic tendencies;
- think through the decision-making process;
- analyze alternatives, anticipate possible issues, and mitigate risks;

- organize a project from the conceptual stage to becoming reality;
- understand roles performed by different participants;
- build enthusiasm and cultivate teamwork;
- develop autonomy and trust among participants;
- persuade nonbelievers into supporting an idea;
- manage time, budgets, and resources;
- delegate, manage, lead, or follow people;
- monitor progress and adapt to change;
- overcome obstacles and objections;
- resolve internal or external conflicts;
- deal with people on different levels;
- handle setbacks and pressure;
- show attention to details.

Sam offered, "I'll give you a comparison.

"On one hand, you can simply say that you're a person who can overcome obstacles and handle pressure, and hope the interviewer believes you.

"Or on the other hand, you can describe an actual situation where you put your abilities to good use.

"Which do you think will make a more positive impression? Most certainly the latter."

An Interview with Intel

To provide an example, Sam told a story to the Go-Getters on their final night in Nepal.

He said, "A university graduate named Danny once interviewed for an entry-level production planning position with Intel.

"Danny studied economics at an upper middle-ranked university, but had no related experience, knowledge of high tech, or MBA. He didn't come from a prominent family and didn't have any connections at Intel. He did, however, possess a fine character, good intelligence, and other desirable qualities.

"In the interview he was asked if he could describe a challenging project he worked on that brought him great satisfaction.

"Danny described a volunteer community service project to underscore his abilities. In his final year at school, he was the project coordinator of the **Special Olympics** for the mentally challenged, an event never before held at his university.

"He explained that he initiated the idea for his university club after participating in a regional Special Olympics. Danny came away from the event with a more mature outlook toward life. He recognized that a similar experience could teach his university club members the same.

"Obtaining approval, however, was no simple task. Some club members were against the project. He eventually overcame the objections and obtained approval from the club president to proceed.

"First, Danny had to get organized. He formed a small committee of other club members to set priorities and plan different components of the project.

"At the same time, he and his committee visited the local school for the mentally challenged to express their wish to hold a Special Olympics. Because they were viewed as being young and immature, they had to convince the school's elder headmaster that their intentions were sincere.

"After obtaining approval from the school, they started coordinating and implementing the project. There were many things to do.

"The committee obtained clearance from the university and arranged use of the campus football stadium. They scheduled athletic events and assigned duties. They also sought food donations from community businesses, planned for a barbecue and awards ceremony, and arranged medical care in case of an emergency.

"During this three-month project, Danny had to be disciplined and organized, since he still had his normal classes and examinations.

"As many things were occurring simultaneously, he also delegated tasks to his committee members.

"Knowing that some club members continued to be uncomfortable with the event, Danny arranged a film of the Special Olympics to be shown to his club a week before the event. This uplifting film helped to convince the nonbelievers that the project was a good idea after all.

"The big day came, with over 150 people in attendance, including the city mayor and university chancellor. By this time, he had 100 percent support from his club members, his university, and the participating school for the mentally challenged.

"Everything went as planned. The athletes enjoyed a fun and memorable event, and the organizers and volunteers came away with a greater outlook toward life. Danny knew that the project was a success and that his efforts had been justified.

"Well, his story must have captivated the Intel interviewer. Not only was Danny's choice of project meaningful, but also he demonstrated a personality rich in character—initiative, discipline, enthusiasm, resourcefulness, organization, delegation, and teamwork. He also showed leadership and community conscience qualities that are greatly in demand by companies today because of the higher awareness of corporate governance and ethics. Altogether, he demonstrated a great attitude and potential to grow.

"When Danny was interviewed, there were other applicants from higher-ranked universities, many with MBA degrees. But it was he who got the job offer.

"Later, the interviewer said it was his story about the Special Olympics—the variety of skills displayed and his good attitude and potential to grow—that convinced Intel to offer him the job."

Sam stressed that while it's great to be the leader of a project like this, those who participate can also display desirable characteristics. As a committee member, individual supporter, or volunteer, one can describe what he or she did to contribute to the overall success of a project, exposing attractive skills and positive characteristics as well.

Sam conveyed that committee members and volunteers of this Special Olympics project went on to become successful partners of top law and consulting firms, doctors, business executives, and entrepreneurs.

For experienced workers, describing a work-related project in the interview is more relevant. Besides highlighting results, summarizing added-value accomplishments would be of great benefit.

"The point is this," Sam summarized. "If you can be associated with an interesting project or organization during your education or while employed, I'd advise you to jump at it. It could prove to be a profound moment in your life and career.

"For an experienced person, it enables you to further underscore your track record. For an inexperienced person, it allows you to convince the interviewer that you have proven abilities to offset your lack of experience.

Describing such an endeavor in a compelling way during an interview provides a great opportunity to highlight your exceptional characteristics and distinguish yourself over your competition."

Chapter 22

Postscript

Go-Getters find success

Over the course of the next month, Sam received e-mail updates from the Go-Getters. They all related the results of their efforts.

He read them, one by one:

- From Toronto, Jeff received an offer to join **Pfizer's** training program, with a plan to move to the marketing department.

- From Miami, Matt joined the design department of **Paramount Parks**, the subsidiary of **Paramount Pictures**—the first step toward his dream of becoming an art director for an entertainment company.

- From Philadelphia, Carl will join the auto parts manufacturer **Delphi** as an internal auditor covering Asia, the initial step toward his goal to move to China.

- From Chicago, Kathleen landed a job at **Kajima Construction** and was assigned to an office building construction as a project engineer.

- From Kansas City, Derek found employment in the **U.S. Federal Reserve Bank of Kansas City** as a research associate with an eye toward becoming a certified bank examiner.

- From New York City, Erica joined the marketing department of **Verizon Communications.**

- From Atlanta, Wendy accepted a research job at **GlaxoSmithKline** in the pharmaceutical and biotech industry.

- From Houston, Heather joined the **Teacher Retirement System of Texas** and will move to Austin to work in the member services department—a solid job that should provide her career stability.

- From Seattle, Sims accepted a job at the **Seattle Times** as a communications specialist, a position that contains a wide variety of future career possibilities in media and PR.

- From Los Angeles, Ann joined **Cisco Systems** as a software engineer to pursue a profession in the Internet telephony industry.

Sam sent back a reply to the Go-Getters:

> Dear Friends,
>
> Wonderful news—I congratulate all of you on your achievements.

I had no doubt that each of you would find success using a market-driven approach. Apply this approach throughout your life—it can continue to help you succeed at work and manage your career.

Now you are starting new chapters of your lives. Here are some final words of advice:

- A positive attitude is everything.
- Maintain your dreams and goals.
- Overcome indecision and go beyond inspiration.
- Continue to be persistent and determined.
- Everyone will make mistakes, including you.
- Keep learning, especially from setbacks.
- Don't let things out of your control hinder you.
- Never stop innovating.
- Maintain open communications.
- Be accountable and preserve integrity.
- Win with humility, lose with grace.
- Be reminded of the gift of giving and gratitude.

Never forget that you're a part of an evolving society that is an embodiment of people just like you. Try to keep things in perspective and maintain sound values and ethics throughout your life.

Show kindness to those people who have disadvantages. Your life will be more meaningful; that's a guarantee. Take note of what Mark Twain said: "Kindness is a language which the deaf can hear and the blind can read."

And as you advance through your career, *don't mistake making a living for making a life*. In other words, maintain balance between family, faith, work, and society. Establish your core values and never stray from them.

Good luck! Enjoy your journey—the rest is up to you.

Sam sat back, smiled, and reflected, "I've got a great job."

The End

Dear All Go-Getters,

We hope this book proves to be a valuable tool in
your quest for career success.

If this book assisted and you've got a market-driven
success story of your job search or career advancement,
let "Sam" know.
Send us a message using our website,
www.sierrapacificpublishing.com

QUICK ORDER FORM

___ **Yes**, I want to order _____ copies of THE GO-GETTERS: Market Driven to Career Success for $13.95 each. For quantity discounts, please call for information or check our website.

___ **Yes**, I am interested in having David A. Lee speak to my organization, school, association, or company.

Your Name: ____

Address: ____

City: ____________________________ State: _____ _Zip: _________

Telephone: ____

E-Mail Address: ____

Sales Tax: Add 8.25% sales tax for orders shipped to California addresses.

Shipping by Air: Please include:
United States: $5.00 for first book, $2.00 for each additional book.
International: $10.00 for first book, $5.00 for each additional book.
Within 30 days of delivery, you may return new, unopened merchandise in its original condition for refund of purchase.

Payment: $ __________ by Check enclosed or by Credit Card:
Please charge my Credit Card: _____ Visa _____ MasterCard
_____ American Express

Card Number: ____

Name on Card: ___________________________ Exp. Date: _________

Signature: ____

Toll Free Telephone Orders: 888-432-1176
Fax Orders: 310-732-1176, or mail this form
and check payable to Sierra Pacific Publishing
28364 South Western Avenue, PMB 463
Rancho Palos Verdes, CA 90275 USA
www.sierrapacificpublishing.com